CHRISTIAN MORAL PRINCIPLES

Seven Sermons preached in Grosvenor Chapel as a Lenten Course in 1921

BY

CHARLES GORE, D.D., D.C.L., LL.D.

Hon. Fellow of Trin. Coll. Oxon.
Lecturer in Theology of King's College, London

WIPF & STOCK · Eugene, Oregon

Wipf and Stock Publishers
199 W 8th Ave, Suite 3
Eugene, OR 97401

Christian Moral Principles
Seven Sermons Preached in Grosvenor Chapel
as a Lenten Course in 1921
By Gore, Charles
ISBN 13: 978-1-60608-265-2
Publication date 11/21/2008
Previously published by Mowbray, 1921

PREFACE

These sermons were not intended for publication, nor were they written; and I know that in my case unwritten sermons are not fit for publication. But they were very well taken down by a shorthand reporter, and I have agreed to their publication, and revised them in a measure for the purpose, because I have some reason to hope they may be useful to others besides those who heard them in Grosvenor Chapel; and also for another reason.

We are told constantly and truly that we greatly need good books on Moral Theology which are something more than adaptations of Roman Catholic books. Now "moral theology" may have different meanings.

1. It may mean the theology or doctrine of God which is required as a postulate for the moral principles and practices of the Christian life. This is a very important subject to which these sermons only attempt incidentally to make a slight contribution, especially sermons iv and v. But it is an important subject of study to which too little attention has recently been devoted. And the utterly irrational idea that Christian morals could maintain them-

selves apart from the creed of the church is still widely current.

2. It may in its traditional sense mean the study on a comprehensive scale and in a scientific spirit of the moral principles of Christian living, individual and social.

3. It may mean the application of those moral principles to particular cases—or what is called casuistry; and it may include the consideration of what is desirable or possible in the way of public discipline by a Christian church over its members who overtly offend against the Christian law. It is impossible to give any serious study to the life of the Christian society without considering the function of excommunication in maintaining the moral standard.

4. It may mean the science of the confessional, that is the application of 2 and 3 to the use of the priest engaged in hearing confessions, and required, often under circumstances of peculiar difficulty, to afford guidance to troubled souls and determine whether such and such a person is a fit subject for absolution.

This special application of moral theology is so urgently required by the clergy that it is apt to be the first thing undertaken. But my own strong conviction is that we need a fresh study of moral theology first of all without any reference to the confessional, simply as it appears in Scripture and history, and as a matter in which priest and laymen are absolutely on the same foundation as disciples of Jesus Christ. To study Christian morals mainly or primarily with a view to the uses of the confessional inevitably, as it seems to me, distorts the study, especially in the Roman Church, where confession is obligatory on all members of the church; it has produced on the whole a quite undue bias towards the consideration of the lowest minimum of conformity to moral requirements necessary for absolution. This is as utterly alien to the spirit of the New Testament as possible. There the Christian ideal is presented not as an "ideal" in the ordinary sense, but as a practical rule of life which Christians must follow. There are special vocations in Christianity, but *not* different moral standards.

I have, then, allowed myself to publish these sermons as an attempt simply to study moral theology in the sense (2) described above, tracing the origin and growth of the moral principles of Christianity in the Old Testament and seeking to interpret them, in their full expression in the New Testament, as a way of life involving certain intelligible principles. This needs doing, however, in a far more thorough and scientific manner than can be attempted in seven short sermons. When this has been done we shall need a book on casuistry, that is a practical application of principles to present day practice—still primarily in answer to the question—*not* what is the least that a man can do consistently with remaining in the communion of the church, but what ought he to do.

5. But there is also another book we shall require before the needs of the priest in the confessional can be properly considered, and that is a book on the right conception of ministerial priesthood in relation to the responsibility and liberty of the individual, and the closely allied practical question whether sacramental confession is to be worked among us as frankly and really voluntary, or as something which, while not absolutely required as a condition for Communion, is still so normal to penitence that one who does not make his confession to a priest is to be regarded as a defective and ignorant Christian.

However, of all these needed volumes these sermons only seek to make suggestions towards the second.

CHARLES GORE.

6 MARGARET STREET,
LONDON, W.1.

S. John the Baptist's Day, 1921.

CONTENTS

	Page
PREFACE	iii

Sermon I
THE WAY. PRELIMINARIES ... 1

Sermon II
THE TEN COMMANDMENTS — THEIR ORIGINAL SENSE ... 14

Sermon III
THE TEN COMMANDMENTS FOR CHRISTIANS ... 31

Sermon IV
HUMILITY ... 48

Sermon V
CHARITY ... 62

Sermon VI
THE USE OF MONEY ... 80

Sermon VII
THE RIGHT SELF-LOVE ... 98

Appendix
THE TEN COMMANDMENTS IN THE CHRISTIAN CHURCH ... 110

CHRISTIAN MORAL PRINCIPLES

I

THE WAY. PRELIMINARIES

"For the people shall dwell in Zion at Jerusalem: thou shalt weep no more: he will be very gracious unto thee at the voice of thy cry; when he shall hear it, he will answer thee. And though the Lord give you the bread of adversity, and the water of affliction, yet shall not thy teachers be removed into a corner any more, but thine eyes shall see thy teachers: and thine ears shall hear a word behind thee, saying, This is the way, walk ye in it, when ye turn to the right hand, and when ye turn to the left."—*Isaiah* xxx. 19-21.

1. "This is the way, walk ye in it." The Bible, Old Testament and New Testament, is the teaching of "the Way": how men ought to live. In the Old Testament the Jews had fallen into the way of their neighbours. They loved religion; they loved the ritual and ceremonial feasts with passionate devotion; but falling into the way of their neighbours they had divorced religion from morality—the morality of common life, of kindness, justice, and

purity. And the Prophets came to teach them the Way: that there is no value in religion except as the expression of the will to live rightly. Of course this involves a theology: a doctrine about God. It is true because the character of God is eternal justice, truth, and goodness, and there is no possible fellowship with God except by loving mercy, doing justly, and walking humbly with our God. That is the beginning and the end; that is the Way.

And when again the religion of Israel was missing the mark, our Lord came, and again He taught the Way to men; and the earliest name for the Church was "The Way."[1] There is no denying that it was a difficult way; it put a great strain upon all the inclinations of men: upon their habits, upon their loved pleasures, upon their wandering lusts and desires, upon their tempestuous bitternesses and animosities. "Strait is the gate and narrow is the way." Our Lord seemed to intensify the severity of God. Nevertheless, so beautiful a thing is perfect goodness, and so terrible the experienced consequences of sin, that our Lord said, "my yoke is easy and my burden is light": that is to them who will take it up with a good

[1] See Acts ix. 2, R.V., xix. 9, 23, xxiv. 22; cf. ii. 28, xvi. 17, S. Luke xx. 21, S. John xiv. 6, 2 S. Pet. ii. 21.

will, a good heart, a good courage. It is a great adventure which requires great courage; but it justifies itself; even as the opposite is the case with the way of lust and self-seeking and sin. You remember those bitter words of William Shakespeare at the end of that tremendous sonnet (cxxix) on lust:—

> "All this the world well knows; yet none knows well
> To shun the heaven that leads men to this hell."

The greatest mistake the church has ever made —and it has pervaded its history—is that of concealing from the young, or from men in general, that Christianity is not an easy thing: it is not a matter of course, which a man may be supposed to accept just because of his position in Christian society, and from which he will not fall away except by some scandalous lapse from the conduct of "a good man and a gentleman." It is hardly possible to exaggerate how widespread has been that misrepresentation, for it lies at the heart of all our evils. No; the Christian life is a way of adventure, a difficult way, a way that requires courage.

Now, in our self-examinations we are apt to examine ourselves about this or that fault which we feel to belong to us, or to be struck now and again with this or that virtue which we see in some one else and which we desire to emulate;

but we have got in our minds no clear image of what the Christian life is in its unity and completeness; and it is that which I desire during these Sundays in Lent to put before you. I am, of course, aiming at being practical; no one can preach about "the Way" without being practical. Nevertheless there is a place for theory; and we Englishmen are apt to forget that. We dislike ideas. If you were suddenly asked, "What is the Christian life? what is Christianity?" you would find it difficult to give an answer. Nevertheless we need to have before our minds a living picture of that difficult but glorious thing—the Christian life and what it means individually and socially. That is what I seek to supply.

2. My second preliminary point is this: the Bible is a great book of development: it has taught the world the doctrine of development. God's ways are gradual; the Bible is a record of a gradual education for a universal purpose or function. God takes this strange people, Israel, which was to be His chosen instrument for the propagation of the true religion in the world: this people so rebellious, so obstinate, but at the same time so incredibly tenacious of ideas with which they have once become identified — God takes this people in a very

The Way. Preliminaries

early semi-barbarous state, and He trains and educates them for the perfect life through His prophets, priests, rulers, kings; and we have the record of the actual stages of this education. It begins in very rudimentary lessons; it is rooted in the Ten Commandments, those short, sharp negatives, "Thou shalt not, thou shalt not, thou shalt not."

Note then, in the beginning of our consideration of the Way the place of the positive and the negative in moral training. No one can doubt that a negative morality is a poor morality. No one can say that the morality of the Old Testament is on the whole negative; for if you take the religion of the Psalms, if you take the glorious visions of the Prophets, if you take the wisdom of the Books of Proverbs or of Wisdom, you cannot possibly deny that there is set before you a great positive ideal. Nevertheless we must never forget that it begins with negatives, "Thou shalt not." And in the Book of Exodus the covenant of God with Israel is immediately associated with "the ten words"; it is based upon them. When the great prophets begin to teach, that is, when we get upon the solid historical ground where we know the dates and the circumstances of the times, their teaching rests on the foundation of the great negatives. They are, as it were, the rough wall which fences in the plot of ground which is to be the garden of the divine and beautiful growth of the perfect life; but there must be this wall, this stern initial exclusion of the things that shall not be.

Psychology is teaching us many things about education, and it starts with the idea that true education must be encouraged to take hold of the natural inclinations and dispositions of the different ages of those who are to be educated. Children are to be taught to love goodness and religion as they would love the birds and the trees and the flowers and everything that is beautiful and attractive. The boy is full of vigour and he is a hero worshipper, and he is to be taught to see in Jesus Christ his Master the great Hero, and to love the attraction and the adventure of His great enterprise. Quite true; all education is a fallacy which is not obviously encouraging, adventurous, attractive. Nevertheless you cannot read modern books about education without seeing that there is a note of disparagement of all that is negative and prohibitory. It is a tiresome feature of human nature that it will ever go by reactions, and that in making any advance it is always apt to exclude by reaction something that is essential, and so to fail of its purpose. I am sure it is doing so in this case. Life—the life with God, the perfect life—is based upon the fear of God; He is formidable because He is righteous; and so it is that there can be no sound education which has not in it the ring of those tremendous prohibitions "Thou shalt not." We must hear the thunder of the voice of God; we must feel that everything that is most to be desired is a garden ground fenced off by those tremendous walls; that there are things that must not be, and to which no toleration ought to be extended. Thus originally, at the basis of all the great structure of the spiritual life, stand the Ten Commandments—"Thou shalt not, thou shalt not."

3. Thirdly among these preliminaries, religion becomes personal to the individual; but it was first of all social: the Way was the way for the nation, the society. Nothing in the world is so false as the old way of thinking, which prevailed in the days of individualism, that men are first of all individuals, and that they afterwards find it useful to combine in society. That was a false theory of the origin of society; it was also a false theory of the Christian religion, that it is first of all for the

salvation of the individual soul, and that afterwards these saved individuals were left to combine in order to form a religious society. The opposite is the historical fact. There was at first, as we have now been taught by all our great historical teachers, hardly any conception of man as existing individually at all. Mankind appears in the world as tribes in which the individual is altogether immersed and lives the life of his tribe, with almost no assertion of his individuality. You see that in the Old Testament. God is a God who makes His covenant with the nation, and who visits the sins of the fathers upon the children to the third and fourth generation of them that hate Him; and, in fact, because there is this continuous social life which we cannot get away from, we do still to-day inherit the punishment of the sins of our forefathers. It was only later that there grew up inside Israel the sense of individuality. You hear the clear note of individuality first in Ezekiel, who boldly contradicts the commandment and says, "The son shall not bear the iniquity of the father, neither shall the father bear the iniquity of the son"; and he asserts in vivid words, through a whole chapter of constant reiteration,[1] the exclusive

[1] Cap. xviii; cf. xxxiii. 10–20.

worth of the individual in the sight of God. And in the New Testament this sense of individuality is strongly emphasized. To Christianity, in fact, we owe the overwhelming sense of individuality: it exists in the same completeness and energy nowhere else: there is the fount of the true estimate of the worth of the individual life. Nevertheless the individual is not an individual except as a member of a society, and "the life" is the life of a society. Even in the New Testament, if you read S. Paul's ethical teaching—those wonderful catalogues of virtues and descriptions of good living—and begin to look at it with fresh eyes, you will see how intensely and profoundly it is a teaching of corporate life. The great adventure is not the adventure of a solitary individual; it is the adventure of a society, the value of which is that it shows the way of living the divine life as men can only live it who are linked to one another in the bonds of fellowship and brotherhood.

4. And then, fourthly, amongst these preliminaries, it is a life to be lived here and now in this world, a life which is to exercise itself and find itself to-day. In the Old Testament, of course, there was hardly any glimpse of a life beyond. That was part of the discipline

of Israel. The nations round about them were largely occupied with the thought of the dead and of the after life: so it was in Egypt, so it was in Babylon, so it was in the nations round about—they occupied themselves in dealings with the dead. But Israel was sternly kept off that ground; it was to know almost nothing about another life hereafter: there is hardly a breath of it till very late in the literature of the Old Testament. They were to learn that God is the living God, making His claim upon them here and now. Only when that sense was developed to its full force were they made to feel that the divine righteousness needed for its exercise a wider world than this, and they began to get their outlook into the world beyond. Of course in the New Testament it is quite different; everything there is calculated upon the scale of the life beyond — an immortal life, an eternal life. Nevertheless, if the true life can find its completion only in that vaster world which is beyond, yet that vaster life which is beyond can only crown and complete the life which is begun here and now. The kingdom of God is to be found in its fullness only beyond the great catastrophe which is "the end of the world"; but the kingdom of God is to be

The Way. Preliminaries

established here and now. What is the church? It is the embodiment of this kingdom of God; it is to be a life lived now amongst the conditions of human society as it stands and humanity as it now is. It is here and now that is its testing ground; it is here and now that it is to exhibit among men what human life can be—to let its light shine before men, that they may "see your good works and glorify your Father which is in heaven." It is to be a present living contact of man with man and man with God; and the discipline of this life begins with these Ten Commandments, which lie in the heart of the great body of Israel's law.

Great codes of law are very ancient. I hold in my hand a book which I should like every one, and especially every student of human institutions and history, to know. I dare say some of you do know it. It is called *The Oldest Code of Laws in the World*.[1] There was discovered just at the end of the last century by the French at Susa a most interesting stone dated and inscribed, and for the most part— except where it had been deliberately defaced — legible and intelligible in the cuneiform

[1] Promulgated by Hammurabi, King of Babylon, B.C. 2285-2242; trans. by C. H. W. Johns (Clarks, Edin. 1903).

script. It is a code of laws which survived in practical exercise apparently longer than any other code of laws has ever survived. It was written and inscribed some 2,300 years B.C. by a great king, who is perhaps the same as is mentioned in the fourteenth chapter of Genesis under the name of Amraphel, among that band of kings who carried off Lot. He is a certain historical character, and we know a good deal about him. We know how he extended his empire from the mouths of the Euphrates and Tigris right across Mesopotamia, Syria, and Palestine to the Mediterranean Sea, in the days of Abraham, hundreds of years before Moses. And on that stone is inscribed, and still legible in the greater part, his code of laws which fills the whole of this little book. It is an extraordinarily elaborate code, and is very like the Hebrew code in many points. No doubt the Hebrews felt its influence, because it permeated the whole of the East. This code, then, was still copied and studied two thousand years afterwards; and it influenced vastly the whole of the East, and it exhibits a very high level of social and legal morality. It goes into great detail; we are told the wages of all the different kinds of workmen five thousand years ago. But if you compare it

The Way. Preliminaries

with the Jewish code it lacks its centre. What distinguishes the Jewish code, or amalgamation of codes, as you get it in the Pentateuch is that it has its centre in these ten short commandments, these sharp, stern prohibitions. The Ten Commandments are given us in the twentieth chapter of Exodus, and in the fifth chapter of Deuteronomy in slightly different form: and if we were able to get at the original form of the Ten Commandments, the form in which they were laid up in the sacred Ark, it is probable that we should find that they were all quite short prohibitions: "Thou shalt have none other God but me"; "Thou shalt not make any graven image"; "Thou shalt not take the name of the Lord thy God in vain"; "Remember the sabbath day to keep it holy"; "Thou shalt honour thy father and thy mother"; "Thou shalt do no murder"; "Thou shalt not commit adultery"; "Thou shalt not steal"; "Thou shalt not bear false witness against thy neighbour"; "Thou shalt not covet thy neighbour's goods." These short, sharp sentences are the fences of the garden of God.

II

THE TEN COMMANDMENTS

"I am the Lord thy God, which brought thee out of the land of Egypt, from the house of bondage. Thou shalt have none other gods before me."—*Deuteronomy* v. 6 and 7; cf. *Exodus* xx. 2 and 3.

As we saw last Sunday, these Ten Commandments—the ten words—these sharp, stern prohibitions, constituted a garden wall to keep secure from alien influences the ground on which the plant of Israel's spiritual and moral life was to grow.

First of all let us take these Ten Commandments as they stand and see what their original meaning was.

(i) "Thou shalt have none other gods before me": that is "in my presence" or "beside me." That does not exactly declare that there exists no other god than Jehovah the God of Israel: though Israel was to learn that higher truth in due course. All that it says is that their worship of Jehovah is to be exclusive: "For you there is to be none other God in my presence." The worship of Israel is to be

The Ten Commandments

exclusive; it is to make no account of any other god. And the same principle is carried out in the second commandment:

(ii) "Thou shalt not make thee any graven image, or any likeness of anything that is in heaven above, or that is in the earth beneath, or that is in the waters beneath the earth: thou shalt not bow down thyself unto them, nor serve them: for I the Lord thy God am a jealous God, visiting the iniquity of the fathers upon the children unto the third and fourth generation of them that hate me, and showing mercy unto thousands of them that love me and keep my commandments." All the nations round about Israel made images of their gods, but Israel was to learn high and spiritual things of God. There was nothing in heaven or earth or under the earth to which God can be compared or to which He can be made like. There must be no kind of similitude of their God—this Jehovah whom they worshipped. And there follow those memorable words about the jealousy of God: "I am a jealous God." Jealousy we think of as a bad thing, as an illegitimate claim which one man or woman makes upon another: a claim of exclusiveness in which there is no right. But there is, even among men, a righteous jealousy.

There is a righteous jealousy of husband towards wife and of wife towards husband. And in God there is a righteous jealousy: there is an exclusive claim which persists even into the New Testament, as when S. James says[1] that the spirit which God has made to dwell in us yearneth to jealousy over us. And this jealousy of God was to show itself in the whole national life of Israel in the sequence of generations: God visits the sins of the fathers upon the children unto the third and fourth generations. As I told you last week, the time came when Israel learned the value of the individual before God, and the reality of His penetrating, rectifying justice to the individual: "the son shall not bear the iniquity of the father, neither shall the father bear the iniquity of the son." That is true: we cannot think of the righteous God unless we think of a discriminating justice as regards the individual. It was that thought which forced men forward to the vision of the life beyond death. Nevertheless the other law remains true. God deals with us as societies of men; and in societies there is no denying the fact that the inexorable righteousness of God works through the succession of generations, and He visits the sins of the

[1] S. Jas. iv. 5.

The Ten Commandments

fathers upon the children, as Israel learned when they entered the deep waters of the captivity.

So these two first commandments claim an exclusiveness for the worship of Israel's God: fencing Israel off from the religions round about them. Theirs is to be an exclusive religion: and the reason is plain to see. The religions round about Israel were nature worships of all sorts and kinds. And it is the way with nature worships that they are non-moral or immoral: for nature seems to show no moral discrimination, and the moods of nature seem to be reflected in the morality of the men who worship nature. So it is that the nature worships of the world have ever been quite non-moral, and where the worship of a tribe or people is the worship of the productive and reproductive powers of nature, there its religion has mostly become positively immoral, and intimately associated with immoral practices. So it was round about Israel; so it is in India to-day. Therefore in order that Israel's spiritual life may grow on intensely and passionately moral lines they are to be fenced off absolutely from contact with the religions of the surrounding nations: the worship of Jehovah is to be an exclusive influence.

Ah! it was not an easy claim to enforce. You know how utterly the commandment seemed to fail. You hear the one long cry of the Prophets, that Israel is abandoned to idolatry and to fellowship with the worship of the nations round about them. And at last God judged them for it. This little people who imagined that they, as the chosen people of Jehovah, could never fail to receive His support, found themselves carried off into captivity, deported into some remote part of Mesopotamia, and all the world said " There is an end of Israel." But the miracle of history took place. They left their land under that sharp judgement, but an astonishing change passed over them. They learnt to hate idolatry and they were brought back in the providence of God to their own land. Thus they fulfilled their destiny, and you can date any document in the Old Testament by whether it shows a fear of idolatry. If it speaks of idolatry as a present danger then it comes from before the captivity. Because in the deep waters of the captivity the whole of that inveterate tendency to idolatry was washed out of them. There were plenty of dangers left: exclusiveness, pride, formalism and other evils; but the danger of idolatry passed away for ever—that is of idolatry in the primary sense. Something of the same kind happened in England. The psychological change in the religious temper of the English people between the middle of the sixteenth and the beginning of the seventeenth centuries was almost as extraordinary. The contrast between Puritan and Catholic England in its whole religious disposition is astonishing.

Then next (iii) this exclusiveness of their religion was to root in the mind of Israel an awful reverence for the name of their God—Jehovah. No doubt they exhibited that reverence in superstitious ways, as by a refusal to pronounce the name: so that they substituted the word "Lord" for the word "Jehovah,' and the word "Jehovah" (or Jahweh) occurs in our English translation very rarely. Nevertheless they were right in reverencing with an awe-struck reverence the sacred name. They might swear by Jehovah, but woe be to them if they took the name of Jehovah in vain for a false or wicked purpose. "Thou shalt not take the name of the Lord thy God in vain: for the Lord will not hold him guiltless that taketh his name in vain." So the great commandment thundered over them.

Next (iv) they were to learn the consecration of their life to God, and they were to learn it from the law of the fourth commandment. "Keep the sabbath day to sanctify it, as the Lord thy God hath commanded thee. Six days thou shalt labour, and do all thy work: but the seventh day is the sabbath of the Lord thy God: in it thou shalt not do any work, thou, nor thy son, nor thy daughter, nor thy manservant, nor thy maidservant, nor thine ox, nor thine ass, nor any of thy cattle, nor thy stranger that is within thy gates; that thy manservant and thy maidservant may rest as well as thou. And remember that thou wast a servant in the land of Egypt, and that the Lord thy God brought thee out thence through a mighty hand and by a stretched out arm: therefore the Lord thy God commanded thee to keep the sabbath day." The seventh day or Sabbath was to be a day of rest. That had the same sort of purpose as the law of the first-fruits or the law of the tithes. The giving of the first-fruits and of the tithes—that is the giving of a small portion of the whole—was to teach them that the whole really belonged to God. So the special consecration of the seventh day, in which they were to abstain from all their work, was to teach them the sacredness of all days. At first it was a simple abstinence from work. Then the vacant spaces of the Sabbath were filled up with the holy meetings for worship, of which we see such rich examples in the synagogue worship of later days. But there was to be first of all this simple abstinence from work. As you know, the law of the Christian Sunday proceeds in the opposite order. It was first of all a day of eucharist, a day of worship; and then, in order that men might have leisure for worship, there was attached to it an abstinence from work, that men might be free for worship. The order of the Jewish Sabbath was the opposite. It was a day of rest from work which became a day of worship.

But as you see, this fourth commandment holds within itself three laws: there is the law of the Sabbath, the law of abstinence from work; there is the law of work for all the other days, "Six days shalt thou labour," which is the root of the Jewish reverence for labour and their contempt for idleness; and then thirdly there is the law of fellowship—the equal regard for the manservant and the maidservant and even the cattle. (We can forgive Eliphaz the Temanite the false things which he said because of the one good thing, "For thou shalt be in league with the stones of the field: and the beasts of the field shall be at peace with thee.") The Jews were to be kind even to their cattle as being fellow creatures of God with themselves; and much more to the people who laboured for them, "thy manservant and thy maidservant." And, as the Book of Deuteronomy gives the motive for the observance of the Sabbath, it was that they had all been slaves in Egypt and God had redeemed them; therefore they must have a sense of fellowship for all who were enslaved and poor. This is the comprehensive scope of the fourth commandment.

Then (v) there follows the fifth of the great distinctive precepts — alone among the Ten Commandments in being positive and not negative—which is the root of all the deep Jewish reverence for the home: "Honour thy father and thy mother, as the Lord thy God hath commanded thee; that thy days may be prolonged, and that it may go well with thee, in the land which the Lord thy God giveth thee." Reverence for parents lies deep in the life of the home. The Jews had a very severe view of parental discipline: there is no question about that. Nevertheless, or for that very reason I suppose, there was no nation amongst whom the sacredness of the home was develloped in so deep and strong a religious spirit as among the Jews; and the commandment tells them that therein was to lie the continuity and the strength of their nation. In their sense of the sacredness of marriage, in their veneration for the procreation of children and their love of abundant families, and in their insistence on the stern discipline of the home—in these things was their strength.

And (vi) "Thou shalt do no murder." They were a fierce people, and there lay deep in their traditions all the instincts of blood feuds. But these instincts were to be disciplined. They were indeed made to learn that "whoso sheddeth man's blood by man shall his blood be shed." The sixth commandment was not an abolition of capital punishment: indeed the Jewish law recognized capital punishment abundantly. Nor was it an abolition of war; for they were still to fight against the enemies of Jehovah. It was not a perfect commandment: but it was a step forward, and it pointed further still: it put an end to the motive of private revenge as a justification for taking the life of a man. There it left them; but it was a fence that made room for better things.

(vii) "Neither shalt thou commit adultery." There again the commandment does not go very far. It is not a general law of purity, but a simple stern prohibition which fences the sacredness of the home by establishing the exclusive relations of husband and wife.

(viii) "Neither shalt thou steal." As you see in the character of Jacob, underhand dealings were very congenial to the Jewish temperament. What Ecclesiasticus called "the sin that sticks close between buying and selling" was very much in their disposition. Again, this commandment does not express anything like the full principle of morality; but it is a stern, sharp prohibition against tampering with other people's property. It was impressed upon them by their prophets, and especially in that sense in which it involves the recognition of the principle of justice and the rights of the defenceless, the poor and the weak.

(ix) "Neither shalt thou bear false witness against thy neighbour." The Jews were a litigious people, and I suppose perjury came as natural to them in law cases as, alas! after all these centuries of moral discipline in this so-called Christian country, it appears to come to us. Therefore the need for this sharp word of prohibition.

Then last there stood that very comprehensive prohibition (x) "Thou shalt not covet thy neighbour's wife, neither shalt thou desire thy neighbour's house, his field, or his manservant,

The Ten Commandments

or his maidservant, his ox, or his ass, or anything that is thy neighbour's." This is a general prohibition of covetousness; a stern limitation upon a man's thirst for more.

So they stand, these "ten words"—these short, sharp prohibitions. They were, as I say, a fence within which was to flourish the rich growth of Israel's spiritual and moral life. And it was a very rich and positive growth. As they were kept away from the fascination of foreign religions and concentrated exclusively upon the worship of their own God, so there grew up among them, under the teaching of the prophets, the glorious spiritual religion of the Psalms—that worthy sense of God's holiness, His goodness, His spirituality: that intense sense of His protection both of the nation and of the individual worshipper, that deep feeling of personal communion with Him, that tender penitence, that courageous confidence, that invincible faith in righteousness, that thrill of exultation at the very sound of the name of God. Is there in all human literature anything more intense, more penetrating, more lovely than the religion of the Psalms? "The Lord is my shepherd, therefore shall I lack nothing." "Though I walk through the valley of the shadow of death, I will fear no evil." "When

I awake up after thy likeness, I shall be satisfied with it." "Thou shalt hide them privily by thine own presence from the provoking of all men: thou shalt keep them secretly in thy tabernacle from the strife of tongues."

The root of idolatry lies in low ideas about God. All the contempt and ridicule which the prophets heap upon idolatry has this for its explanation. So it was that worshipping a God of whom there could not be in the region of visible things any similitude, the mind of Israel was lifted to conceive of Him, in His spirituality, His omnipresence, His holiness and His love, with an adequacy to which no other nation on earth made any approach. And as He had made Jerusalem His home, and its Temple the scene of His special presence, there developed itself that unique and passionate patriotism, centring in the city and the temple, which was only another aspect of their religion and their worship.

Again, the penetrating sense of the righteousness of God which inspired the prophets of Israel provided a basis for a positive social conscience, which far transcended the limits of the Ten Commandments. Where among ancient peoples can we find anything like the sense of truthfulness or the sense of justice which grew in Israel? "Lord, who shall dwell in thy tabernacle, and who shall rest upon thy holy hill? Even he, that leadeth an uncorrupt life : and doeth the thing that is right, and speaketh the truth from his heart." Where is to be found elsewhere such a positive loathing of all cruelty to the weak and all "grinding of the faces of the poor" as we find in Israel? "Now for the comfortless troubles' sake of the needy, and because of the deep sighing of the poor, I will up, saith the Lord." And not only in the prophets and psalmists do we find this strong sense that God is against every tyrant, but in the sober common sense of the "wisdom literature"—the Books of Proverbs and Ecclesiasticus.[1] Do not forget, moreover, their reverence for manual labour[2] and their contempt for all idleness, luxury, and vice. Surely the positive religion of Israel, the plant which grew within the sacred enclosure of the Ten Commandments and the Law, was a growth of incomparable glory.

No doubt it was imperfect. We may note this in three respects. First, it was on the whole limited to their own people. The mind of an Isaiah, and of some others of the prophets,

[1] See Ecclus. xxxiv. 20-22; xxxv. 12-17.
[2] Ibid. xxxviii. 24 ff.

from time to time is visited with the vision of a world-wide fellowship of all nations in God—a fellowship in which Egypt and Assyria should be one with Israel—but on the whole, even in the best of the nation, the sense of the loving purpose of God was limited to Israel, and the rest of the nations were viewed as the enemies of Israel and the subjects mainly of the divine judgement. Secondly, there was a very inadequate sense—very inadequate, that is as measured by the standard of Christ—of what the redemptive mercy of God can accomplish in seeking and saving the worst and most abandoned. Thus they gave over the wicked to the divine vengeance much too readily, and carried into their private enmities the eager claim for the divine chastisement upon those who had done them personal wrong. The claim of the maledictory psalms is based no doubt upon a profound truth, but it falls surely very far short of the Christian sense of the mind of God towards even the worst offenders. For this reason surely Psalm cix had better not be recited in the public worship of those who have been taught by Jesus Christ. It requires too much explanation.[1] Thirdly, though there are

[1] I would have the whole Psalter retained for the private recitation of the clergy, but certain omissions made in its public recitation in the general congregation.

some glorious estimates of womanhood in the Old Testament, yet here again—in the position assigned to women—we are on the whole far below the level to which our Lord has raised us. It is of the essence of the Old Testament to be imperfect. As you wrong the Old Testament, says S. Augustine, if you deny that it comes from the same God as the New, so you wrong the New Testament if you put the Old on the same level with it.

There is only one word which I will add. The Bible is of all books the most contemptuous of majorities. This is true of the Old Testament as of the New. The true religion, the religion of the prophets and of the Psalms, appears as the religion of a faithful remnant who hardly maintain their ground among a faithless people. This is true especially of the period before the captivity, but the same estimate of the relative moral force of the few and the many appears also in the later books. Thus in fact when He came upon whom the hope of Israel centred, the Christ of God, the vast majority of the nation rejected Him. The true Church of God, the true Israel, is found, after S. Paul's preaching, to be made up mainly of Gentiles. And this should be our encouragement. The struggle of the true prophets and of the faithful Israelites to maintain what the mass of the nation regarded as an impossible standard justified itself in the result. So the like struggle always justifies itself. It is the best who keep the world from corruption. It is when the best men cease trying that the world sinks back like lead. Let us never lose heart in maintaining the full moral truth—the fullness of the divine claim. It is the perfect goodness which men really reverence, even if they have not the courage to follow it. It is always worth while to maintain and follow the best.

III

THE TEN COMMANDMENTS FOR CHRISTIANS

"From that time[1] began Jesus to preach, and to say, Repent: for the kingdom of heaven is at hand."—*S. Matthew* iv. 17.

The New Testament is founded upon the Old, and the link between them is John the Baptist, the last of the prophets of the old covenant, who points to the new; and his message—his Old Testament message—is that the kingdom of God, the kingdom or reign of God or of heaven, is at hand. This kingdom or reign of God means that world in which the will of God has complete sway; in which the hearts and wills of men are in agreement with God; and in which accordingly all the true glory of human life, which sin and wilfulness had effaced, is again manifest, and God comes into His own. You will recall the heart-rejoicing descriptions and pictures given in the Old Testament of that kingdom of peace and glory. Now then it was at hand; there was

[1] That is, the time when John the Baptist had compulsorily ended his preaching through being cast into prison.

to be no more delay. That was the word of John; that was the word which, from the lips of John, Jesus proclaimed when he said "Repent ye, for the kingdom of heaven is at hand."

As the teaching of Jesus developed it appeared that this kingdom or reign of God had a double sense. In its perfection it lies beyond this world of struggle and conflict; it belongs to the time of "the world to come," when God in the whole universe of things is to come into His own and there is to be no rebellious will; the day when Christ shall come in the glory of His Father with the holy angels—that is the consummation. But our Lord also manifestly speaks of the kingdom as something already in process: growing as the mustard seed, leavening the world like the leaven in the lump. And it is in this aspect that the kingdom is in some sense identified with the Church. For the Church of Jesus is the instrument and exhibition of the kingdom; that is its purpose and mission: it is to exhibit in our world, which both admires and hates it, a society of men in which the kingdom of heaven holds sway, and the true lineaments of the transformed human life are made plain. That is what the church is for: to show the kingdom

The Ten Commandments for Christians 33

of God as already in being among the men of to-day. Therefore "Repent ye"; because the requirement of entering into the kingdom here and now is the same as the requirement for entering into the kingdom of God and of Christ in its perfect manifestation hereafter. And the world as it stands "lieth in the evil one." Its lust and selfishness and wilfulness cannot come into the kingdom of God; it is utterly alien from it; therefore there must be a fresh beginning. "Repent ye, for the kingdom of heaven is at hand."

How deep the needful repentance must be is made evident to us when we notice our Lord's attitude towards all the different classes of society. There were the leaders of religion, the Pharisees, who upheld a high and exacting standard of religion and conduct in certain respects; but they were hard formalists, exclusive, unmerciful; and it is upon them that our Lord pronounces His most tremendous maledictions—it is upon the ecclesiastical world, and the leaders of the ecclesiastical world, of His day. And there were the Sadducees, the nominal priests and the real politicians, occupied with their worldly politics, upon whom also He turns His back. And there were the common people who heard Him gladly, and gladly received the outpouring of His miraculous bounty, but who were occupied with their nationalist aspirations or their ordinary cares, so that but few of them listened to the real meaning of His teaching. So it was but a little band which would make the great surrender and enter upon the great adventure, and to them—overheard indeed by others, but for them in the first instance—that He spoke His Sermon on the Mount.

He begins His sermon with a vivid description of the ethical character of the kingdom in the Beatitudes. Among these there stand first three great paradoxes. "Men are everywhere hunting for money; but I say blessed are the poor; if not the poor in fact then at least in will and heart; blessed are the detached. Again, men are everywhere hunting for pleasure; but I say blessed are those who enter into the sorrows and sufferings of the world; blessed are they that mourn. Once more men are everywhere asserting themselves and putting themselves first, but I say blessed are the meek."

But it is not only in negatives that our Lord describes the character of the kingdom; and the positive descriptions of the Christian character which follow attract even those who

The Ten Commandments for Christians 35

are not willing to make that character their own. There is the hungering and thirsting after righteousness or the passion for the good —no mere formal righteousness but a positive passion for the good; and the mercy and the purity or singleness of heart, and the love of peace, and the readiness to suffer. And this character, so unworldly, so isolated from the world, but so rich and ennobling in its motives, is to stand there in the midst of a bewildered or hostile world distinct in itself, like salt to keep the mass from corruption; manifest like the light shining in the dark place; raised evidently aloft like a city set on a hill. Then our Lord passes on to revise the Ten Commandments; because we are not to think that in being in one sense free from the letter of the law, or free from all those manifold enactments with which the Pharisees burdened the law, we are to be allowed to rest upon a lower standard. No; "except your righteousness exceed the righteousness of the Scribes and Pharisees, ye shall in no case enter into the kingdom of heaven."

So He takes the sixth commandment, "Thou shalt not kill," and with a divine authority He revises it. Henceforth in His kingdom the first allowed movement of anger, which is the root of murder, is to hold the same place of seriousness in human judgement as murder had hitherto held. And this feeling of antagonism and hatred when it passes into words of bitterness and contempt, because now more deliberate, is still graver sin and is subject to severer judgement. You see He presses back the moral requirement behind the fully accomplished outward act to the first movement of the will and the first expression of passion.

Then He takes the sin of adultery: "It was said to them of old, Thou shalt not commit adultery; but I say unto you, that whosoever looketh upon a woman with the view to lust after her hath committed adultery with her already in his heart." Our Lord's meaning is precisely this, I think; that the deliberately-conceived intention of sinning, though it be restrained from actually taking effect, has all the sinfulness and the guilt of the outward sin. It is all a matter of the will. Therefore a man is to go to the very depth of his being, and where he finds something in himself that is a hindrance to true spiritual freedom, or control over his passions, he is at all costs to exorcise it and cast it out, even if it be, as it were, a part of his very being, because a man must be strong at the centre before he can be free at the circumference of his being. Thus Jesus said, "It is better to enter into life halt or maimed rather than having two hands or two feet to go into hell."

Once again He takes the third commandment. "It was said to them of old time, Thou shall not forswear thyself"; that is, one could put himself at certain moments into the presence of God, and swear by Him, and thereby claim a special sacredness for that particular word. All that was required was that he should keep this specific oath. But God is everywhere; heaven is His throne, the earth is His footstool, Jerusalem is His city; there is nowhere where God is not; you are always in His presence. Therefore the sanctity formerly attending on special oaths is to attend on the whole of your conversation. "Let your yea be yea, and your nay nay." That is, truthfulness, universal and deliberate, is the duty of one who knows that the presence of God is everywhere, and that everything said is of the nature of an oath in the presence of God.

Here, in the opening of the Sermon on the Mount, we have given us a tremendous rectification or transformation of the Ten Commandments from the outward act to the inward motive, from the negative to the positive.

Indeed the Christian transformation of the Ten Commandments is very thorough.[1] It is not only that the second commandment is transformed by the Incarnation, because, God having manifested Himself in the acts of the human life of Jesus, we are permitted to exhibit in picture or symbol these visible incidents of the life of God in the flesh for our remembrance and our edification. It is not only that the fourth commandment is transformed from the law of the Sabbath to the law of the Lord's Day. But also the other commandments—the third, the sixth, the seventh, and the others—are transformed from negative to positive, and from commandments of the outward act to commandments of the inmost motive. There is no wonder, I think, under these circumstances, that the early church was shy of erecting the Ten Commandments into a position of prominence, as if, standing by themselves, and pronounced in their original form, they could be the moral law for the Christian. It is a remarkable thing that until the thirteenth century the Ten Commandments were never erected, with the Creed and the Lord's Prayer, into the class of things which every Christian

[1] I have endeavoured to give some detailed account of "the Ten Commandments for Christians" in *The Sermon on the Mount* (John Murray), App. ii.

must learn and know. I am not now attempting to criticize the position which the Ten Commandments have traditionally held in our services and in our preparation for Confirmation.[1] But certainly, if they are to hold such a position as that assigned to them among us, at least let us recognize how deep the conversion which they need, and how disastrous it is if we take them in the letter and not in the full richness of their inward spirit.

Well then, this glorious and inspiring, but tremendous, picture of the true life—this law of the kingdom of God—our Lord proceeds in manifold ways to expound and illustrate, not only in the Sermon on the Mount. It is illustrated by His example, and it is expounded in His parables. And His parables in various forms bring out this thought, that whatever faculties of man are seen to be efficient and powerful in the business of common life—all his watchfulness, forethought, prudence, and intellectual application—are to signalize the children of the kingdom also. There is to be nothing left out; there is to be the fullest exercise of all human faculties for the supreme purpose of the kingdom. Later of course the

[1] But I am reprinting, as an appendix to these sermons, such a criticism "The Ten Commandments and the Christian Church" from a volume called *Dominant Ideas* (Mowbrays).

Christian character is the main theme of the Epistles of Paul and James and John and Peter; and indeed there is nothing in the world more lovely than the descriptions of the Christian character given us by these different but accordant teachers.

I shall have the opportunity, please God, on successive Sundays to illustrate different aspects of this character; but what I want to plead for with you to-day is this: that you should set yourselves this Lent to get before your minds, as you can do if you read continuously the Gospels and the Epistles, a clear image of what the Christian character is Godward, selfward, manward. It is your duty to God to love the Lord your God with all your heart and with all your mind—with mind as well as heart: that is, to get and to keep true ideas about God, for our Lord knows that how men behave will depend at the bottom on what they really think about God. God, then, is love; not less severe and uncompromising in His righteousness than the old Prophets proclaimed Him; not less severe than the God of Amos; but shown to us now in His intense love. And this love is not merely a quality of His own internal being, but goes out, energetic and passionate, to seek and save every one of the wandering children of men who are lost in their wilfulness, their malice, or their lust. It is a love which knows no limits, which extends over the whole area of human life and from which no wanderer is outcast. "I came not to call the righteous, but sinners." Thus those most contemned by the respectable world—the publicans and harlots—may even be in a better position before God than the proud and the contemptuous, because they are more open to the divine appeal. And our Lord made it quite evident, though He was sent only to the lost sheep of the House of Israel here and now, yet He made it quite evident in His dealings with individuals, as you heard just now in the Gospel,[1] that it was man as man, quite irrespective of race or class or kind, that the love of God was ever seeking with infinite self-sacrifice: for in Jesus Christ it is a self-sacrificing, suffering God who is evidently set before our eyes. And now that God's real character and purpose has thus been made manifest in Jesus Christ, it is never to cease to be manifest before men; for the purpose of His kingdom, His church, is to make it continually manifest. And the one object of "the children of the

[1] The Gospel for the Second Sunday in Lent—the story of the woman of Canaan.

kingdom " is to be conformed to the heart of God. That is what the church is for; it is to keep alive among men this sense of what God is, both of His righteousness and of His love; and as the child of the kingdom looks out towards God that is the one concentrated desire of his heart—to be so truly a son of God as to be conformed to His mind.

This is our duty towards God: and therefrom follows our duty towards ourselves. Our duty towards ourselves is prudence; it is to make the best of ourselves; and to make the best of myself is to make myself a suitable citizen of His kingdom and a suitable member of His household. Therefore I must purge myself from lust and selfishness and malice, and see to it that my will has full dominion over my passions and appetites; therefore I must see to it that all my faculties are exercised, and that I make the best of every power I have. Because to save my soul means just this: to make the best of my faculties, as one called into the fellowship of an eternal kingdom, from which all that is morally alien must be perforce excluded.

And my duty towards my neighbour is to recognize to the full that in God's sight every man counts for one, and no one counts for more than one; that every single human soul has an absolute and an identical value in the sight of God; and that He will tolerate no contempt or selfishness, no using of other men as instruments for our own comfort or our own aggrandisement; but that the spirit of brotherhood must pervade our every relation to our fellow men.

For fellow sharers in the spirit of Jesus that is the ideal of life: that is its outline. It is a lovely outline surely, and, though it is a tremendously severe claim that is laid upon us, yet at the same time it allures us by its incomparable glory.

Brethren, is it not true that even at our worst and most perilous moments we recognize in our deepest hearts that there is nothing in the world for any human being so glorious as this treasure of Christian character; nothing so royal, nothing so priestly, nothing so worthy to enlist our faculties and our wills? Well then, I would implore you first of all to set it clearly before yourselves. That is the first thing—conversion; that is the turning of our hearts deliberately to choose the best: feeling sure that, whatever the cost, that cost is reasonable; determined to follow no other pattern; resolved deliberately to make this great purpose ours.

But you may say—Strive after this ideal for myself I certainly will; but I am afraid really to put this ideal forward before others; it is too high a standard. If I put this before my sons or daughters, or before the world at large, I shall only alienate them. Surely there are two standards: there is the high standard which a man should entertain in his private heart, but for the world at large there must be a much lower standard. I want to tell my children that they must behave as good and honest men and women, and keep themselves from those scandalous sins which are a recognized disgrace. Surely we must have this lower standard—the conduct of a gentleman —for use of the world. If I put the high standard of Christ before people in general I do nothing but alienate them.

What am I to say to this plea? Truly I believe that the acceptance of the principle of a double standard has been a disaster which lies at the heart of all our economic and social troubles. It is the exact opposite of the method of Christ. Do not misunderstand me. Our Lord had a great reverence for what we should call natural goodness. "Thou art not far from the kingdom of God"; He loved to say that. He noted with gratitude the smallest acts of kindness and goodness. A cup of cold water given only in the name of a disciple He said should by no means lose its reward. A bruised reed would He not break, and smoking flax would He not quench. We should never forget that. The most ignorant attempts to do good He valued. "He who is not against us is with us." Jesus really loved and valued natural goodness. And further towards every man who was trying to follow Him, like His apostles, He was full of supreme mercy; no number of falls and failures can take us out of the scope of His forgiving goodness. If our wills are right, He is always ready to set us free to begin again; indeed perseverance is nothing else but a succession of fresh beginnings. Jesus is indeed a generous and merciful Master.

But as regards the standard of the kingdom —that which He could accept and welcome into His kingdom—He would have no compromise. History it seems would have been wholly different if He would have accepted a lower standard as the standard of positive requirement for His kingdom. It was because He so uncompromisingly claimed the highest that He seemed to fail. And yet, mark you, He is really justified, not only by the supreme justification of His authority, but also by experience. For, as He said, what keeps the world from rotting is the standard of the best. And the standard of the best, believe me, is not unattractive. A real Christian is magnificently attractive. Only I beseech you, never let any one for whose education or guidance you are responsible, think that Christianity is a matter of course or that a person can be a Christian just by avoiding scandalous conduct. Never let your sons and daughters imagine that they can be Christians without a tremendous act of choice. The notion of Christianity is a matter of course, or that a person can be counted a Christian who is not guilty of some scandalous violation of decency, has no sanction in the Gospel. There are no two standards for the kingdom of heaven; the only standard for that kingdom is the one which I have been trying to describe and which is gloriously human and divine. It is the standard for all; and, believe me, we have at this moment a great opportunity. There is in the world to-day a very widespread revolt not only against the doctrines of theology but against the Christian standard of life. For instance, you can see the world rising in open rebellion against the Christian standard of purity; or again against the Christian standard of self-denial, or of spiritual equality. Man's lusts, man's passions, man's avarice, man's pride are to-day in very open rebellion. This open rebellion gives us our opportunity. For the world will inevitably find out its mistake. Its selfish passions will be its destruction. What is wanted in the midst of the bewildered world is the witness of the true life visibly being lived by an organized society of men—the witness of The Way. That is the only effective witness. There can be no regenerating power in the midst of our society except through the restoration of the true standard as Christ proclaimed it—so plainly, with such infinite variety of expression, with such fullness of human sympathy, and with such tremendous severity of claim.

IV

HUMILITY

"Yea, all of you gird yourselves with humility, to serve one another: for God resisteth the proud, and giveth grace to the humble. Humble yourselves therefore under the mighty hand of God, that he may exalt you in due time."—1 *S. Peter* v. 5, 6, R.V.

Let us return to the consideration of the Christian character somewhat more in detail.

I think that any one who sets himself deliberately to contemplate the Christian character in its completeness and the variety of its lineaments cannot but receive a profound impression. Here is something so satisfying to our whole sense of perfection, and so liberating to all our faculties and capacities, that we feel that it must be real, that is, in accordance with the real nature of things. Thus it seems to us that the doctrines about God and about man, which are its inseparable accompaniments or grounds, are proved to be true by their practical value; "so that," in Shakespeare's words,

"The art and practic part of life
Must be the mistress to this theoric."

So I would have you come back to the contem-

Humility

plation of this "art and practic part of life"—the Christian character as it is to be practised; and in particular to-day to that which is one of its most salient characteristics; that is, its glorification of the virtue of humility.

The word or idea of humility was not new; but in the Roman Empire, into which Christianity came, it was almost, though not quite, uniformly associated with notions of servility. It was a servile quality—bad, therefore, rather than good in its associations. But Christianity lifted it at once into the position of supreme dignity and supreme importance. "He that exalteth himself shall be abased, and he that humbleth himself shall be exalted."

That weird but brilliant modern philosopher Nietzsche, about whom we used to hear a good deal at the beginning of the war, revived, as I daresay you know, the theory that humility is a servile virtue; that it is the virtue of weak and common men, who, having successfully combined to glorify it, have thus kept down the superior man, the super-man, who for his proper elevation and due self-realization needs to be able to despise the common herd and treat them with the contempt they merit. Well, I do not suppose you read Nietzsche, or are particularly liable to be influenced by him;

but I fancy, as one looks round on human life, one seems to see a depreciation of the idea of humility, as if it were associated with something low and servile, which extends a great deal more widely than any knowledge of Nietzsche. Humility does not appear to be a popular or highly-appreciated virtue to-day. I think that there are a great many people who practically appear to think that it is a servile quality which they had better get rid of. It is associated with weakness and ineffectiveness.

And yet it is, perhaps, a sufficient argument against such a position to point to the beginnings of our religion, and especially to those two figures who stand upon the threshold of Christianity as the prominent examples of humility, whom yet no one would call servile. I mean John the Baptist and Mary, the blessed mother of our Lord. John the Baptist was essentially humble. You see his humility in his indignant protest when flatterers or admirers would have ascribed to him some excellence or some pretension which was not his. Perhaps, they suggested, he was some supernatural person, Elijah risen to life again, or the predestined prophet, perhaps he was even the Christ. Well, every powerful preacher is surrounded by flatterers, and you know how John the

Humility

Baptist received them; it was with an indignant and reiterated "No, I am not." And when they turned upon him and asked in what then lay his right to baptize, he said, "I am the voice of one crying in the wilderness, Prepare ye the way of the Lord." After me cometh the Greater One. That is humility. Humility utterly repudiates pretentiousness; it bids us love the truth about ourselves; it stands upon the solid rock of truth. Therefore it is at the point furthest removed from servility; for what makes people servile is that they care what other people think about them. If you live mainly in the light of what other people think about you, then you will be indeed at times arrogant and at times servile, according to the people you happen to be with. But if you stand simply on the rock of reality, in the light of what you are in the sight of God, you can never be servile; you will stand as John the Baptist stood and speak the truth to powerful and common people alike. You "can no other."

Or again, think of Mary. She was the very type of modest retiring womanhood. Would you call her servile? No. Once she sang a song, and that *Magnificat* of Mary reveals nothing of servility. No one can read that psalm and fail to see that Mary was royal-hearted, and entered into the fullness of God's great purpose for His people, and understood the dignity and glory of being the instrument of His purposes. The great S. Bernard, who speaks much about this virtue, gives us the true account of it. He was a man of incomparable force, and wielded great power in Europe. He was also a man of humility, and knew what it meant. He advocates it constantly. He says, "Humility is the truth about ourselves." So it is, both Godward and manward.

Godward it is the recognition first of all of our absolute dependence upon God who created us, so that everything I am and everything I have at every moment depends upon Him. If at any moment He were to withdraw from me the breath I breathe or the life by which I live, I should sink into the nothingness out of which I came. Absolute, unqualified dependence is the truth of my condition, and whatever difference there may be between the greatest and the lowest among men or among creatures, that difference at its utmost is as nothing to the difference between the creature and the Creator. Thus I think that humility deserves, with faith, hope, and charity, to be called a theological virtue, because it depends upon that doctrine of the Creator which is distinctive of Christianity.

Christianity came into a world which, so far as its intelligent members were concerned, believed in the one God as the divine reason pervading all things, of which the reason in man is a part. Each man, in his reason at least, is a part of God—so they believed. These fragments or sparks of God in us are at present united to the defiling qualities of the material body, but at last, after whatever defilement and pollution, they are bound inevitably to return to the great whole of which they are parts. This doctrine, which we call the Higher Pantheism, can never be the basis of a doctrine of humility. If we are parts of God—if God depends upon these parts of Himself, and upon me amongst them, as much as we depend upon God ; if both are necessary the one to the other as parts of one whole—truly we shall never be humble ; we shall never have in ourselves the root or ground of humility. Humility depends upon the doctrine of God the Creator; that He made me wholly, and that I am utterly dependent upon Him and not He in any respect upon me ; that I am purely His creature, and not a part of Him. This truth bows me down to the earth. Pride in an utterly dependent creature is consummate folly. "Is not this great Babylon which I have builded?" So Nebuchadnezzar said in his folly, forgetting his utter dependence. "Soul, thou hast much goods laid up for thee for many years"; so said the rich man in his self-satisfaction. And the answer of the Bible is, "Thou fool." For what hast thou that thou didst not receive and that thou dost not hold moment by moment at the hands of God? Thus the position of the greatest of men is in the face of God abject enough. As a man I lie at the feet of God absolutely prostrate: I can raise no protest against Him. "The Lord gave and the Lord hath taken away; blessed be the name of the Lord." "Not my will, but thine be done." But all this self-prostration is but the other side of our supreme exaltation; because God who made me, made me a reasonable being, made me to be a son of God, a participator in His purposes, and vicegerent of His counsels. He gave me the lordship of will and reason. He made me to co-operate with Him. Thus the glory of divine fellowship which lifts me to the very throne of God, high into the heavenly places in Jesus Christ, is but the other side of that prostrate humility which is the recognition of God who made me.

And so again humility is the truth about ourselves with regard to one another. I dare say you remember the famous line of Homer in which the Greek hero describes his ideal for his son, "Always to be the best and to be superior to other people." Now of that ideal the first part is Christian and the second part is anti-Christian. The first part is Christian— "always to be the best." It is the most solemn duty of every Christian to make the best of himself in body, soul, and spirit, because he is wanted; God has willed to entrust to him part of the carrying out of His purpose. That is what I am here for; therefore it is my sacred duty to make the very best of myself in every one of my various members, qualities, and capacities, so that I may be as fit an instrument as possible for doing God's will. We might be every one of us infinitely more worth having than we are, if we would eradicate our harmful vices and incapacities and diligently improve ourselves as instruments for God. To be the best therefore—the best possible—to be satisfied with no inadequacy which is removable, no limitation which need not be ours—always to be the best, should be our constant aim.

But "superior to other people"? No. The ambition to be better than some one else, to excel some one else, though it is ingrained traditionally into our habits of education, is, I take it, at the root always pagan, wicked, and misleading. It is suggested to us by these day-dreams to which we may apply Isaiah's words, "This shall ye have of my hand; ye shall lie down in sorrow."[1] Yes, I am apt to compass myself about with day-dreams when I am young; and the essence of these day-dreams, I fear, is always vanity. It is the hunting field I am thinking about if I walk in the country, and it is I who am taking the fences and I who am in at the death. Or it is the enraptured audience, but it is I who am singing the song. Or it is the thrilled congregation, but it is I who am preaching the sermon. And this sort of desire to excel other people—the determination to be the first, as distinguished from the determination to be the best—is always an evil thing to be extirpated. God loves me and made me because He loved me, but He has no preferences. He does not love me better than any one else. He desires that the community of man should serve Him with their variety of faculties, and the best that every one can do is demanded for the full exhibition of what God would have men be.

[1] Isa. l. 11.

Humility

Therefore I must rejoice in my own gifts and also in the superior excellencies of other people. That is what humility means—that I have no desire to pull down others that I may have my head above them. Humility is totally without jealousy or envy or greed of others' excellencies. Nay, rather, it marks those words of Peter's which I read to you for my text, and it goes back to that scene of the Last Supper where Jesus girded Himself with the towel like a servant to wash the feet of Peter and the others. Yes, Peter, using the very remarkable word "gird yourself with the servant's apron," bids us serve our brethren, rejoicing in nothing so much as the opportunity of ministering to the weakest and the smallest. Humility is the love of service; and that mankind may be the richer, it delights in the excellencies of others as much as in its own. It has no desire to depreciate its own capacity, and still less has it any desire to depreciate the capacity of other people; it is the simple truth about oneself with a joyful regard to the excellencies of others. Such is humility.

And yet I must go one step further, because there is a further demand which (for example) S. Paul makes upon us. He not only bids us not "think of ourselves more highly than we ought to think," but further he says, "Each esteeming others better than himself," "in honour preferring one another." And he calls himself the "chief of sinners." All this is worthy of our attention; and it is very characteristic of the saints. But we feel at first sight as if there was something unreal about such language. We quite understand equality of consideration, but not this self-depreciation by comparison with others. Perhaps, after all, I am better than somebody else in fact, and I ought to recognize it. There is a good deal of this feeling lurking within us—that the language of the saints in self-depreciation is unreal.

Now humility would still be the truth about ourselves if there were no sin in the world and no sin in us. But I think it is the consciousness of our sin which makes this language of self-depreciation natural. No doubt, judged from any external point of view, S. Paul was not the "chief of sinners"; but, on the contrary, one of the greatest of the saints. But there is also no doubt that S. Paul spoke the truth about himself from the point of view of his own feeling, and that is the particular note of the consciousness of sin. I can never estimate other people's sins, but I can estimate my own. S. Paul could estimate what it was to have so long persecuted the church of Christ, and it made him feel that nobody could have been so bad as he was. And that as a feeling is right and just. I am able to estimate my own sins, and I know what they mean. I know how I have thereby insulted God, injured my fellow men, enfeebled my capacities, and polluted my best gifts. I know how in myriad instances, which pass all number, I have defeated the purposes of God and defiled the very atmosphere of my life, and harmed others as much as myself. Thus on some particular occasion in life I may be unjustly treated, and get less than, as it seems to me, I deserve to have. But there is no moment of my life in which I can fail to recognize that if I were to get my deserts on the whole, I should be where lost souls are. Therefore the sinner who knows himself is always prepared for the lowest place. That is what all the self-depreciatory language of the saints means. I cannot estimate other people's sins, but I can estimate my own, and I know where they would place me.

There is only one other word I would add. S. Bernard, whom I have taken as my guide, is very fond of using sentences of this kind: "We are all humiliated, but we do not all become humble."

We are all humiliated. Experience is very humiliating probably to every single one of us. Ah! those day-dreams that I allowed myself to indulge, kindling a fire and compassing myself about with the sparks that I had kindled! But experience has been very humiliating. Of all those great plans how little has been realized! Of the great things I intended to do what a little has been actually accomplished! Thus it is that life is a very humiliating retrospect to almost all men. Yes, we are all humiliated; but it is a great question how we take this inevitable humiliation. We do not all become humble. To a vast number of people it has the effect of something simply distressing, discouraging; turning them into dispirited and discontented men and women; lowering their ideals, leading them not to expect much of themselves or of any one else; making them cynical, bitter, discouraging to young ideals. You know the kind of picture of a middle-aged man or woman that one could easily draw. Their cynicism they are pleased to call wisdom. No; we do not all learn humility; for humility is a joyful, happy thing; humility is fellowship with God constantly renewed in hope. Whatever may have been my faults and my follies I can always start afresh. Humility confesses its sins and takes from the unmerited goodness of God the fullness of His free forgiveness, and, like a child, is happy again, ten thousand times over happy again; joyful in the sense that God loves me, joyful in the sense that He gives me over and over again my fresh opportunity; and however old I am He helps me, though it be but to walk the last day of my life in the fullness of my joy and the freshness of my opportunity. Brethren, our experience of life will certainly be humiliating; let us be careful that humiliation shall teach us humility.

V

CHARITY

"Beloved, let us love one another: for love is of God; and every one that loveth is begotten of God, and knoweth God. He that loveth not knoweth not God; for God is love. Herein was the love of God manifested in us (or 'among us'), that God hath sent his only-begotten Son into the world, that we might live through him. . . . Beloved, if God so loved us, we also ought to love one another."—1 *S. John* iv. 7-11.

If you set yourselves steadily to consider the Christian Way—the principles of Christian living—two virtues or qualities present themselves as fundamental, pre-eminent, and essential. Humility is the first, and the second is charity or love—the two words being but the different translations in our familiar English Bible of the one Greek word "agape," which was a word, you may almost say, coined or minted in the Christian church—the most distinctively Christian word.

Now, I suppose there have been days when men found it possible to talk about the principle that God is love, and the consequent duty of loving all men, as a sort of commonplace. But those days, I think, have

Charity 63

gone by. Intellectually we recognize to-day how difficult it is to believe that the Force which lies behind, and works throughout, the development of the universe is pure and unqualified love. And I fancy that if you talk to sincere people about the consequent duty of loving all men, you will find that to most it presents itself as something that is impracticable. They know—or think they know—what love is. They love some people and not others: that is, they like some, and they dislike others. But the root of their mistake is that they think of love as a matter of emotion or feeling. Now no doubt we cannot directly control our feelings; we like some people and we dislike others: that is a fact. But we can learn to love the people we do not like. That is a large part of Christian duty; and, as I say, the root of our common mistake is that we have thought about love too much as a feeling, whereas in fact Christian love is a matter first of all of our will and intelligence.

If you ask me what Christian love is, I would say it is deliberate correspondence with the declared purpose and mind of God. That is it. The root Christian principle, incomparably the most difficult, and also the most attractive, of Christian dogmas or doctrines, is the doctrine that God is love; which is not an obvious truth by any means, but is the central point of that positive self-disclosure of God which the Bible conveys to us, and the central meaning of the incarnation of God in Jesus Christ. The meaning of the Incarnation is, I say, that the real character of the being who made and rules the world has been for us translated out of that difficult and unintelligible region of abstract things beyond our sight into the intelligible lineaments of a human character which all can understand, the character of Jesus of Nazareth. I do not deny for a moment the intellectual difficulty of the doctrine. It is easy to believe in divine power, for that is manifested everywhere in nature; it is easy again, in a certain sense, to believe in divine righteousness, for on the whole that is declared in the human conscience all the world over, and the threat of its tremendous judgements is felt upon us. But love —that the mind of the being who made and rules the world is absolute love, and His mind towards every single individual pure goodness —that in this full sense God is love, is something so astonishing and so contrary at first sight to much of our experience, that we can only have real or adequate grounds for believ-

Charity

ing it, if we believe that in the human character of Jesus Christ we get the real and express image of God who is His Father.

I am not now going to argue the abstract principle; but I would say to any one here who feels a fundamental doubt on that subject, that you may, and indeed you must, argue the matter in your own mind, and you may get some relief from argument; but ultimately I believe you will find that the real settlement of the question lies only there where you confront yourself deliberately and steadily with Jesus Christ and hear His solemn affirmation that He alone has the right and authority to speak about the nature of God: "No man knoweth the Father save the Son, and he to whomsoever the Son willeth to reveal him." You cannot fail to note that He continually emphasises one thing as the supreme and all-essential truth, and it is that God is the Father of all alike, which is what S. John expresses in the phrase that God is love. And I fancy there are very few of us who can deliberately at the last resort turn our backs on Jesus Christ and say frankly "I do not believe you."

But, as I say, I am not here to-day to argue that abstract question, but only to seek to show you where lies the significance of the word of

Christ. Because undoubtedly, if this is the truth—if the ultimate law of the universe, the law of the very being of God who made the world, is love—if that is creation's final law—then every reasonable person must perceive that he has one summary duty, which is to correspond with the purpose of the world or the summary law of nature. For the ultimate folly is to be out of harmony with the fundamental law of being. Every one knows that. And just as lust or pride puts me out of harmony with the purpose of the world, so exactly in the same sense selfishness, class narrowness, jealousy, malevolence, indifference —these things allowed to become characteristic of my life—put me utterly out of harmony with God and with His purposes for me. Observe, indifference and selfishness do this quite as much as active jealousy or active hatred. Our Lord was at pains to make that emphatic. It was indifference—the ignorant indifference of those who looked at the suffering of the world and said it was not their fault, which He so solemnly declared would exclude men from His kingdom. "Lord, when saw we thee sick or in prison and did not minister unto thee?" And the Lord said "Inasmuch as ye did it not unto one of the

Charity

least of these my brethren ye did it not unto me. Depart ye cursed." Indifference or selfishness, either the willingness to accept the sufferings of others as a matter of course which we can ignore, or the willingness to treat any other human being as simply an instrument of my convenience, puts me utterly out of harmony with God, because the love of God is not the mere abstinence from doing mischief; it is an active, positive, and persistent quality which can never cease to seek and save the lost or the miserable. In fact no one can have any doubt about what the love of God means if it is expressed in the character of Jesus Christ, and if that is truly the law of the world.

Thus the first beginning of real deliberate Christian living is steadily to contemplate what God is ; and to resolve that my life is going to be deliberately so lived as to be in harmony with God. Is our thought of heaven and hell? Well, heaven is communion with God ; and hell is to be out of fellowship with God ; and there is no possibility of evading the conclusion that to suffer a character of selfishness to be built up within me, or in that most expressive phrase of Isaiah, to "hide myself from mine own flesh"—to let the natural advantages of wealth or position screen me from the sufferings of the average man—that is deliberately to build up a character out of harmony with God. Selfishness or indifference is hell self-made within me. That is the truth; and it is a most momentous moment in my life when I realize it. And on the other hand, the acceptance of the Christian law of love is the realization that I must be in harmony with the law of the universe or the being of God, and the being of God is love.

Let me go on to emphasize the breadth and universality of this quality of divine love; because, as I said, in a sense we all love; we love our friends, our relations, our families; we all have a natural sympathy with our class; there is a sphere within which we respond easily to the demand of those who are about us. But the point is that this sort of natural predilection, natural love, is exclusive, it is narrow; it has natural sympathies and it has natural antipathies, and it has almost indomitable prejudices. There is nothing to choose between class and class in this respect, or between nation and nation; they all have their loves and they have their hatreds, their sympathies, and their suspicions. We talk a great deal to-day about the conflict of capital and labour. Who can say that one class is in this respect any better than another class? Each class has its natural prejudices. Their sympathies are narrow and sectional, like our personal feelings towards one another—there are people we like and people we dislike; and it is this narrowness that distinguishes them from the quality of divine love which has that strange and masterful impartiality which will admit of no restraint. That is the point. In Jesus Christ there can be neither Jew nor Gentile, neither male nor female, barbarian, Scythian, bond nor free, because the principle of Christ's dealings with men was to refuse such limitations. That is apparent. The love of God is impartial and universal; there is no single human being whom God created for any other reason than because He loved him, and truly wills his good, and proclaims him redeemable, a possible son of God, made for sonship and communion with Him. On that basis and principle the Christian church was built.

I have said it often, and I will say it again: the Christian church was in the early days compelled by circumstances to show what it meant by love and brotherhood in the sphere of its common social and industrial life. In those days Christianity was persecuted, disliked, and distrusted; and the fact that it was so kept it pure. No one can have become a Christian who was not prepared to suffer for it. Thus, as you read in the Book of the Revelation, they were boycotted by the industrial society about them. It was the will of society that men should not buy or sell with them. And moreover, they on their side were compelled to stand apart, because they found the whole industrial and social world saturated with forms of idolatry from which they kept themselves puritanically aloof; thus they were thrown in upon themselves, and were compelled to build up a social and industrial life of their own. And in spite of manifold moral failures they did it so impressively that the world said with astonishment, "See how these Christians love one another." For the first time in human experience men saw what a great organized brotherhood of men of all kinds and classes really meant. They had their maxims or principles of social organization. First, that every man must be a worker: "if a man will not work," they said, "neither let him eat"; secondly, that every man who would work had his full claim to maintenance, his full and equal claim to the conditions of a man's true life. So the Christian church set itself to find work for all its members; and if it could not find a man work, or if a man was too ill or too old to work, it found him maintenance. And thirdly, that it might have means to do this, it laid it down as the law of justice that no one had any right to retain for himself more than was necessary for his own proper support and that of his family; so that the rest of his possessions must go for those who had nothing and who could not otherwise be provided for. Thus there was built up a society in which the rich became poorer, and the poor became richer, and every member recognized the claim upon him of every other; and the world saw the marvellous sight and said, "See how these Christians love one another."

Now we know something of the vicissitudes through which the church has passed since the days when it became fashionable to be a Christian and there was no longer any selective principle to keep it pure. In particular we know how after the Reformation in England, when ecclesiastical authority had been almost destroyed among us—that is the authority and tradition of the whole catholic society—there built itself up in England and in other countries an industrial system in the making of which

Christian principles had been allowed no say; a system which was based confessedly on the then dominant philosophy of selfishness, that is upon the principle that man is naturally an acquisitive animal and that industrial society must be based upon the principle of selfish acquisitiveness. It was supposed that you have only to set free this acquisitive principle in free competition, and you will build up a society which will be progressive and (it was supposed) free, on the basis of free competition. For a long time we were quite triumphantly pleased with this ideal, and with its results. Now we have been disillusioned. You can hardly read any careful thinker to-day without seeing how far this disillusionment has gone. You can hardly speak to a thoughtful business man who will not tell you that industry cannot go on on the basis of this everlasting conflict between competing interests and between capital and labour organized as natural enemies. Our statesmen tell us exactly the same thing about international life—that we cannot go on upon the basis of the irreconcilable conflict between nations, each pursuing its own selfish end. So we found our schemes for a new fellowship among nations, and men dream of a new industrial society which shall be based on the

Charity 73

fundamental principle of the equal spiritual value of every single human soul, and upon the universal duty of work and the service of the whole community by each of its members.

But we are also painfully conscious that we have no means of effecting the difficult transition from the one basis of social organization to the other. We contemplate the future with the gravest alarm. Men's heads are failing them for fear. Our civilization, as we read almost every day, is in the balance. Can the desired transition be effected without a revolution, we ask? And if the revolution occurs, what will it lead to?

I have recalled to your minds these anxious questionings of to-day only because I want you to see that the real question is whether men in sufficient numbers in every land and in every class will agree to live by the divine law. The root of all our trouble is that we have substituted for the divine law, "Thou shalt love thy neighbour as thyself," a quite opposite maxim or set of maxims as the basis of our industrial and our international life. The question whether the structure of our civilization is to totter and fall seems to me to be at bottom the question whether men will return to recognize and seek to obey the law of God, or how many men in our society which calls itself Christian will seriously do this. If not, as the prophets and our Lord tell us, we must fall under judgement.

But of course it is not merely a public question; it is a private question also. S. John would have us test ourselves rigidly in the matter; and my sincerity is to be tested not by my abstract assertion of principles but by my manner of dealing with individuals in want or those whom I do not like, or those who have done me some serious wrong. For observe it is a matter of act or will and not of feeling. Love, I say, is of the will or heart. I understand that some one has done me a wrong. But do I take pains to understand what God's thought and intention is for him, and what God would have him be? If so, I may have to be severe, but the severity will be utterly purged from the motive of revenge or the desire to see him suffer. It will become simply an expression of the pure goodwill of God. I must think it out; I must be quite deliberate. When I have forgotten myself and fallen into the old bad failings of temper and spite, I shall think it out again. And in the long run your feelings will follow your will. In the long run, although it may not be until after many years, you will

Charity

feel towards a person as you deliberately choose to act towards him.

And then, lastly, I am to see the principle of love as it is set before us in Jesus Christ. I see in His life and teaching that love means active service according to my opportunities; that I must eradicate out of the very foundations of my being the idea that I am justified in living to enjoy myself. In the same way I must seek to eradicate it out of the heart of my family, as far as I am able to do so. I sin if I allow boys or girls of mine to grow up with the idea that to enjoy themselves may naturally be the governing motive of their lives because they belong to a privileged or wealthy class. I am sinning the deadliest sin if I let myself—or as far as lies in me let any other—fashion life on that principle of living for enjoyment. I live for service. Do you say that that is a gloomy view of life, because service to Jesus meant sacrifice, meant suffering? Well, I fully acknowledge that it is a tremendous thing to recognize that we are to take up our cross and follow Him. He does not guarantee us against suffering, even the extremest suffering. By this we are to mark the reality of our service, that we are ready to suffer even to the death. And I suppose this sounds less strange now than it did before the war. We learnt again in that particular sphere, what war is so powerful to teach, that service does mean sacrifice. "Greater love hath no man than this, that a man lay down his life for his friends." But it is comparatively easy to learn that in war; it is extraordinarily difficult to learn it in peace. But I entirely refuse to admit that the view of life as service is a gloomy view: and also, without depreciating the quality of suffering, I am quite sure that we think wrongly, if we allow ourselves in any way to be tinged with what is a purely pessimistic and not a Christian doctrine, that there is any value in pain for its own sake. If you look at the life of Jesus Christ you will notice the fact that out of the thirty-three years of his mortal life thirty years were passed in what I suppose was human happiness. He lived in a happy, well-to-do home amidst friends. There is no note of grave suffering suggested to us with regard to these thirty years. I know what that great book of the *Imitation of Christ* says, that He was never for one hour without the pangs of His Passion. But I cannot see the slightest ground for that statement. I say that, as far as we have any reason to know, thirty years of those thirty-three years of His mortal life were passed in natural simple happiness. Moreover, He never appears as seeking pain, with perhaps two slight exceptions. He did fast, it is recorded, forty days and forty nights. And He did refuse the drugged wine which was offered to criminals before their crucifixion, choosing to have all His human faculties about Him during that supreme suffering. But with these two exceptions I think I may defy you to find any sign in our Lord's life that He sought pain for its own sake.

The pain of Jesus deepening into anguish, deepening into the Cross, came solely out of the double root of obedient service and sympathy. He set Himself to obey without compromise the will of the Father who had sent Him. He set Himself to service—the service of every one of His brethren, and He set Himself to sympathy. He spread out all the broad spaces of His human heart that men might lay their suffering and needs upon it. The suffering that came upon Him came purely, simply, and inevitably out of that obedience and service and sympathy in the world as He found it. And that is the law that I would set before every child—the desire of service, the willingness to serve, the self-equipment for service. But there are none of us too old to learn it. Granted the resolute will of obedience, the resolute self-equipment for service, granted a large-heartedness of sympathy which refuses to be bound by the limits of family or class, then, I say, there will be abundant joy in life. Indeed a well of fresh-springing joy has been opened, and it will be in the providence of God to settle how much of suffering and how great acuteness of suffering shall come upon us. That there will be suffering there is no doubt. The mark of suffering is the mark of Christ; and yet what we seek is not suffering, it is service; but when the suffering comes we shall be ready for it.

The point from which I began and at which I end is the challenge that Christ offers to you that you should organize your life to co-operate with the wide love of God, and not let it drift. Let it drift, and it will drift upon the lines of selfishness and class narrowness, tempered no doubt with wider emotions, but always dominated by the old narrow current. Organize your life then on the basis on which every reasonable man must desire to organize it—that is the basis of the mind of God; and you know what God is, as you see Him in the face of Jesus Christ. The mind of God, the mind of Him who made and rules the world, is the mind of love that is universal and without qualifications; and in this and no other way shall all men know that we are children of God and Christ's disciples, if we have love one to another.

VI

THE USE OF MONEY

"And Jesus looked round about, and saith unto his disciples, How hardly shall they that have riches enter into the kingdom of God! And the disciples were amazed at his words. But Jesus answereth again, and saith unto them, Children, how hard is it [for them that trust in riches][1] to enter into the kingdom of God! It is easier for a camel to go through a needle's eye, than for a rich man to enter into the kingdom of God. And they were astonished exceedingly, saying unto him, Then who can be saved? Jesus looking upon them saith, With men it is impossible, but not with God: for all things are possible with God. Peter began to say unto him, Lo, we have left all, and have followed thee. Jesus said, Verily I say unto you, There is no man that hath left house, or brethren, or sisters, or mother, or father, or children, or lands, for my sake, and for the gospel's sake, but he shall receive a hundredfold now in this time, houses, and brethren, and sisters, and mothers, and children, and lands, with persecutions; and in the world to come eternal life. But many that are first shall be last; and the last first." — *S. Mark* x. 23-31.

The Christian use of money is a difficult subject. I am not going to talk to you about political measures or schemes of industrial or social reconstruction. I am going to try and speak to you solely about the attitude of the Christian soul towards money. And what I

[1] The words in brackets are doubtful.

The Use of Money

desire of you as you listen and think is purely and simply this—as unprejudiced and detached an attitude as possible ; that is the disposition of people who honestly desire above all things to be real and faithful disciples of Jesus Christ.

We cannot read the Bible, Old Testament or New Testament, honestly without becoming conscious that there is therein a tremendous suspicion of being rich ; a tremendous suspicion of riches as such ; though the Old Testament and the New Testament are different. There is a great deal of truth in the saying that prosperity is the blessing of the Old Testament and adversity of the New. In the Old Testament there is at least one strand which takes prosperity and wealth, national and personal, to be the mark of the divine blessing. And you have in the Old Testament plenty of good rich men with the blessing of God on them. Abraham, Boaz the landowner, Job at the beginning of his story and at the end : for the author insists on making him rich again at the end. And there is that wonderful picture of the rich woman householder in the last chapter of the Book of Proverbs, "who openeth her mouth with wisdom, and the law of kindness is on her tongue, who looketh well to the ways of her household, and eateth not the bread of idleness." Nevertheless there is another strand; there is in the prophets a profound suspicion of wealth and its effects. So in the social law which is contained in the Pentateuch you find the main object of great groups of regulations is to protect the poor from the rapacity of the rich. That, you may say, is stamped upon the social law of Israel among its main objects. Thus you find laid down the obligation of the Sabbatical year, that is every seventh year, when the fields were to lie fallow and their natural produce was to be free for the poor, and when debts were to be remitted. And you have the jubilee year every fiftieth year when almost all property was to return to its original owners.

It is very difficult to say how far these laws were actually enforced or obeyed; plainly over long periods they were quite ignored; so that you get in the Prophets and Psalms page after page of terrible denunciation of the rich—of the people who desire to enlarge their properties at all cost, to "add house to house and field to field," who "hide themselves from their own flesh," that is, seek to be exempt from the ordinary sufferings of their fellow men; and their greediness, their oppressiveness, their grinding of the faces of the poor, and their

The Use of Money

luxury are denounced, as you know, scathingly and mercilessly, and they are held up as the main objects of divine judgement, remorseless and terrible.

Further when you come to the New Testament and ask about the teaching of our Lord, you find this same suspicion of wealth as such. Our Lord chose His disciples, or apostles, among the poor; and He looked round on them and said "Blessed are ye poor; woe unto the rich." We must not misunderstand His words. He had chosen His disciples among what we should call well-to-do workers. There was nothing sordid or servile about their condition. They were independent fishermen, many of them, of the Lake of Galilee, owning their own boats, some of them having their own hired servants, living a hard-working life of manual labour, but reaping the produce of their own labour; leading lives without any element in them of servility or dependence on any one else, in frugal comfort, as we should suppose, without fear or favour of superiors—anything but a servile condition of poverty. And then they had made what was the great abandonment. They had given up all they had to become the disciples of Christ, and they moved about with Him, but still in no servile or sordid position. They had now no property; they lived upon what people gave them—those to whom they preached the kingdom — or what was brought by that little band of women who accompanied them and ministered to them of their resources. If you go to India you would still find that an almost normal phenomenon is that of the teacher, a religious man moving about among the people, without property or supplies, and gladly and willingly supported by those among whom he moves. There was nothing servile, then, about their condition.

But certainly our Lord had a suspicion of wealth; He had a suspicion of whatever allowed people to feel themselves a privileged class, or conduced to their regarding themselves as exceptional people who counted in God's sight for more than their fellows. So he had a suspicion of the learned class; but it expressed itself more often concerning the rich class. They would be the people who would instinctively feel that they were a privileged class, and that other people were to work for them; and it is upon that kind of feeling that He pours His tremendous irony. There are no two utterances of our Lord more tremendous than the parable of the Rich Fool and the parable of the Rich Man and Lazarus. There is nothing nearer to contempt to be found in our Lord's words. I wonder how many of you have read the famous sermon preached in All Saints', Margaret Street, not far from here, by Dr. Pusey about fifty-six years ago on "Why did Dives lose his soul?" There was no more startling sermon preached in the process of the Tractarian Revival, and it ought not to be allowed to perish. It spoke nothing but the truth. So it was that our Lord welcomed continually manifest and open surrenders of wealth. That is what He suggested to the rich young man, who went away saddened thereby and reluctant. He proposed to him that he should give up all that he had and follow Him; and, short of that, you remember how the rich man Zaccheus, who held the obnoxious position of publican or farmer of the Roman taxes, when he was converted and subdued by his nearness to our Lord, stood out and made public profession of what he was going to do in the future. "Behold, Lord, from henceforth I give half of all I make to the poor; and if I can find in the past any wrong that I have done to any man, I hereby declare my intention to restore it fourfold." And this hearty act of renunciation Jesus met with His emphatic benediction. He loved these acts of renunciation, and He required the like act of renunciation from those who were to be His apostles. So when you move forward out of the Gospels into the Acts still you find these constant acts of renunciation. It is the habitual atmosphere. So great is the spirit of brotherhood that they had all things in common. There was no legislation to that effect; it was entirely voluntary. But these acts by which people sold their property and brought the produce and laid it at the apostles' feet for general distribution were common.

You go on and you think about the teaching of S. Paul. S. Paul is not at all a communist; he knows how to abound as well as how to lack. It is very difficult to resist the impression that S. Paul was well off in the latter part of his life, as we should use the words well off. But yet he is very severe concerning wealth. He says quite at the end of his life that "godliness with contentment is great gain, for we brought nothing into the world, neither can we carry anything out." What does it matter, then, whether we lose it or keep it? What we want is the spirit of being content with little —really content and satisfied. "Having food and covering we shall be therewith content. But they that desire to be rich fall into a temptation and a snare and into many foolish and hurtful lusts, such as drown men in perdition. For the love of money is a root of all kinds of evil . . . therefore charge men that are rich in this world that they be not high-minded nor have their hope set on the uncertainty of riches, but on God, who giveth us all things richly to enjoy . . . that they be ready to distribute, willing to communicate."

If you go forward again out of New Testament times into the times that followed, and study the atmosphere of the early Christian Fathers which I sought to describe to you last Sunday, you will find a tremendous claim laid on wealth. There is a recognition of the law of private property as a necessary condition in the world — necessary in its fallen condition, necessary in a world of sin. But this law of private property is to be overshadowed by the law and principle of justice; and the law and principle of justice is that every man has a duty and right to work and to receive support adequate to his need; "from each according to his capacity to each according to his need." And the people who have more than they need, and hold it back from those who have less than they need—who refuse to distribute—are not merely uncharitable, but they fail to follow the law of justice, and the Fathers do not scruple to say that they steal what they selfishly withhold. That is the spirit of the Fathers.

Now let us pass over the whole intermediate time and think of our condition as we know it to-day. In the early days they were quite full of the principle that covetousness—and the Greek word means simply the love of getting, the mere desire to get more, the desire to be rich—covetousness is idolatry; it has taken the place, that is, of the old desire to worship idols. There was substituted for that literal idolatry the worship of mammon; the placing of wealth in that position in the heart where God, His will, His love, and His justice ought to reign alone. Covetousness is idolatry. But now think of our tradition. This desire to be rich, (Is it not the plain truth?) instead of being in our minds as one of the chiefest of sins, has come to be regarded as one of the most natural and legitimate of all desires, and the becoming rich up to the limit of his powers and opportunity as the normal ambition of every man? I do not think I can be said to be exaggerating. We have consecrated the very thing which is denounced in the first days. It is honour, instead of pity and contempt, with which we have surrounded the ambition to get rich. I do not think it is possible to deny this; and it is a tremendous ethical change.

Or again, if you look at our law—the law which was built up during the period which is generally called the great industrial epoch, and which still more or less holds its ground—you are struck by one thing: that it enormously accentuates the law of private property, making it as unrestricted as possible, as against the protection of persons, which is much less carefully guarded. It is remarkably the opposite of the law of the Jews in that respect; its main motive is the protection of property rather than the protection of persons. If you think it out, I fancy you will find that this is indisputable. And the result has been a condition of society in which is presented a vast gulf between the rich and the poor. And in the condition of the poor, mark you, the main cause of misery and disaster has been, not so much the actual amount of wages received, as the sense of dependence upon others, and the consequent insecurity and continual dread of unemployment. If you know anything about those whom we call "the workers" you will always find that at the heart of their discontent, and their reasonable discontent, is that profound sense of insecurity. And everybody is agreed that the condition of things as we have it now, and the consequent spirit of hostility in which the different classes face one another to-day, is so profoundly disastrous as to threaten the very basis of our civilization.

Well now, I do not want to leave this matter without practical suggestions. As I say, I am not going to talk about laws or methods of industrial reconstruction; but what I want to ask for from you is a certain disposition or deliberate attitude of mind on this subject of wealth, and to ask it in the name of Christ.

1. First, I would ask that it should be frankly recognized that to live and to enjoy one's self in idleness on the toil of others is a totally illegitimate position. Of course I recognize to the full that there are many different kinds of labour, and that the owner of property who really manages his property is labouring; and a man who thinks and studies and writes is labouring quite as truly as any one else and quite as hard; and a woman who manages a household or brings up a family is doing the noblest kind of work. By all means let us broaden our sense of what work means. Nevertheless, "if a man will not work neither let him eat." No man or woman grown to

maturity has a right to eat his dinner or her dinner unless he or she earns it; unless he or she feels honestly "I have done the work which deserves this dinner; I am a worker who is receiving my necessary sustenance." Now I believe it would be an immense transformation of our society if the children of what we call the upper classes had this truth ingrained into them. I do not so much mean by particular lessons given to the young—though such lessons might well be given—as by the whole assumption of society; because as I look back upon my own school days, I feel that any such assumption was infinitely remote. We had, most of us, no doubt at all that we were a class for whom other people were to work and who were to enjoy ourselves to the best of our opportunities. We too might have to work: nevertheless there was no doubt that we were going out into life to get as much enjoyment as we could, and that, as a matter of course, other people were to work for us. And I do not think that spirit is at all dead, and it requires very fundamental eradication. Every boy and girl must be taught that he must justify his existence by labour profitable to society, and any one who fails to do this should be made ashamed of himself.

2. Then, secondly, I am sure that we need to make a great effort of detachment from wealth, and to learn again the old Christian fear of being rich. We must revive the belief that if we have got what is necessary for our maintenance as far as we are concerned—food and covering, and the necessities of healthy life—we have got all that we can reasonably claim. "Having food and covering let us be therewith content." There may be more laid upon us. We may have larger responsibilities; we may have riches; but we must cut ourselves free from the desire to be rich. And there would follow, no doubt, from that new attitude towards wealth what our society greatly needs—that is public instances of the voluntary abandonment of possessions. There are perhaps more instances amongst us to-day of such abandonment of wealth and property, where it can legitimately be renounced, than people are aware of; but there is no public opinion that welcomes them and rejoices in them. That is what we need; then they would be both more abundant and would produce more spiritual effect. Of course there will remain many people who have the responsibilities of property and wealth, and who cannot renounce them. Nevertheless it would be

The Use of Money

a great thing if we were detached. Our Lord said, "Blessed are ye poor"; that is those who really and voluntarily have nothing of their own; but besides that He said, "Blessed are the poor in spirit"; that is those who are detached from money and the desire for money.

3. And then, thirdly, we need to think fundamentally about the meaning of justice and about the relation of justice to the rights of property. Justice is a divine thing; it means a certain equality among men: not equality of faculty or equality of position or status, but a fundamental equality none the less. It means the equal right of every single man and woman to have the opportunity to make the best of himself or herself. That is a very radical proposition; yet I am sure that the great Christian church has been right in its best days, in finding here the real principle of justice in the sight of God, before whom certainly every man counts for one and no one counts for more than one. This principle is no enemy to the rights of property in a certain sense. Christianity is not communistic. I cannot conceive a healthy society without private property for use; that indeed seems to me to be involved in the independence and

nobility of the individual life. But an almost unrestricted right of property is a very different thing; and I do claim that our almost unrestricted right of property is hostile to a very fundamental Christian principle. I used, thirty years ago, to have more to do than I have now with certain attempts to reform or rebuild slum property. The unrestricted right of a man to keep property which was injurious and simply a source of widespread degradation —seemed to me then and still seems to me to be an intolerable evil. And yet not only was that right practically unrestricted, but you could not even find out who the people were who owned the property in the various stages of ownership. They could effectually conceal themselves. Again, that what is confessedly a dangerous trade, like the trade in intoxicating drinks, should be allowed to pursue its way with so little regard to what is obviously the public interest, but simply for private profit —that I think is a fundamental and disastrous betrayal of the welfare of society.

We need to reconstruct our whole conception of the right of private property so as to see that it ought confessedly to be restricted and limited by the general interest. Perhaps we have improved in this matter of late years,

The Use of Money

but there is a great deal of room for improvement still. We need to feel again, with a quite fresh vividness, that the welfare and dignity of persons, the value of every single human life, ought to be a prior object in the eye of the law as compared with the right of property. Money, in fact, is a trust and a responsibility before God for the general good.

Thus I am quite sure that no Christian ought to be able to invest his money in any concern, without a very bad conscience, unless he has done his best to assure himself that that in which he proposes to invest it is for the public good. Nor can his responsibility end there. His conscience ought not to allow him to retain money in investments without, up to the limits of his power, ascertaining from time to time that his money is being rightly used, and taking what measures he can to protest, if he have reason to believe that it is not being used for the common good. I have in my own small experience found out that even insignificant shareholders can do something by protest, though they represent but a small body of opinion. The point is that we cannot make or retain an investment without responsibility for the use, as regards the general welfare, that it is being put to.

What a tremendous injunction it is that our Lord lays upon us in that parable of the Unrighteous Steward, where He studies the wisdom of the unscrupulous world, and bids the children of light to imitate it for their own purposes. "Make to yourselves friends out of the mammon of unrighteousness"—that is out of money which is generally being used for bad ends, "that when it fail, they may receive you into the eternal tabernacles." Use your money in such a spirit as to make to yourself friends in eternity who shall welcome you into everlasting tabernacles! That is an astonishingly searching maxim for the use of money.

I ask you, then, to think of those three points: the absolute and peremptory duty of every one to work for his living, in some line of profitable labour—bodily, mental, or spiritual; the duty of detachment from the love of wealth and contentment with the necessaries of life; and the realization of the law of justice as overshadowing the rights of private property and directing our responsibility for the use of our wealth.

Looking out over the surface of society to-day we all recognize the extraordinary peril with which our civilization is threatened, and that through the pursuit and use and

The Use of Money

distribution of wealth, unregulated by the motives which Christ, our Master, would make effective. It is in His presence we get and spend. It is to His searching judgement that we are subjected. And I am sure that we can best serve as well the interests of our society as the welfare of our own souls by a very diligent exercise of our stewardship as in His sight.

VII

THE RIGHT SELF-LOVE

"Or are ye ignorant that all we who were baptized into Christ Jesus were baptized into his death? . . . For the death that he died, he died unto sin once: but the life that he liveth, he liveth unto God. Even so reckon ye yourselves to be dead indeed unto sin, but alive unto God in Christ Jesus. Let not sin therefore reign in your mortal body, that ye should obey the lusts thereof."—*Romans* vi. 3, and 10-12.

It is the fashion at the present moment to disparage the religious anxiety to save our own souls. The hope of heaven and the fear of hell are by our modern prophets widely decried or disparaged as selfish and unworthy motives. But this is really neither scriptural nor sensible, because after all there is a right kind of self-love. I never like the modern substitution of "selflessness" for unselfishness. For the self is a divine reality, and we are bound to preserve it. The golden rule is "thou shalt love thy neighbour"—not instead of thyself but—"as thyself." In fact the instinct of self-preservation is not a sin or a defect, but a fundamental and God-given instinct, inherent in everything that has life, and most of all in that which

The right Self-love

has the highest kind of life—in the soul or self of man. And if it be possible, as our Lord so solemnly and repeatedly warns us that it is—if it be possible by wilfulness, carelessness and sin fundamentally to ruin our very selves, our very fundamental being, and if hell means the state of those who have thus finally and fundamentally ruined themselves, there must come over any one who chooses to think a shivering horror at the awful possibility which lies before him — a horror which must, by the very constitution of human nature, become a motive for avoiding with all deliberate care the kinds of action which lead to self-ruin. Moreover, all experience shows us that it is only this care for our own souls which can enable us to fulfil our function in society. How many public careers, which might in greater or smaller degree have been careers of public usefulness, have been destroyed by private sins! How many undertakings, which might serve a useful purpose, are baffled and sometimes rendered impossible by the private jealousies, obstinacies, uncharitablenesses, ambitions of this or that individual! S. Paul was quite right, when he was exalting the glorious privilege of being a fellow worker with God, to go on at once to speak of being studious to avoid private sins, of giving diligence that his ministry be not blamed, lest his service of God be thwarted by obstacles interposed by his own defects. From every point of view we need the most diligent care of our own souls, for truly our own soul is a trust. Do you remember those poignant verses of John Henry Newman, at the head of which he inscribes "the zeal of Jehu"?

> "*Thou* to wax fierce in the cause of the Lord,
> To threat and to pierce with the heavenly sword;
> Anger and zeal and the joy of the brave,
> Who bade *thee* to feel, sin's slave?
>
> The altar's pure flame consumes as it soars;
> Faith meetly may blame, for it serves and adores.
> Thou warnest and smitest! yet Christ must atone
> For a soul that thou slightest—thine own." [1]

It is very hard to be a good Christian. We inherit, so the Christian doctrine tells us, a fallen nature. I will not enlarge upon that, save by saying that all experience seems to verify the doctrine. It is not only progress we need but redemption; and our redemption was purchased for us at a tremendous price. Not with corruptible things such as silver and gold were we redeemed, but by something of inconceivable value, even by the precious blood

[1] *Lyra Apostolica*, lxvi. This volume seems to me to let us into the secret of the Tractarians more fully than any other.

The right Self-love

of Him who sacrificed Himself that we might live. How can we then take our salvation lightly? Surely we must, as S. Peter says, "pass the time of our sojourning here in fear."

I am now going to speak of this zealous care for our own souls from one point of view: a point of view which in any series of sermons which professes to deal with Christian moral principles cannot be avoided; I mean the sexual appetites of mankind. I daresay if we knew each other better we should know that we are all equally tempted in one respect or in another, taking all temptations into view. But certainly with regard to this particular temptation we are not all tempted equally. Nevertheless the average man and woman in all classes of society is warned by many experiences that these sexual appetites, which in the providence of God belong to our nature and are His appointed means for the propagation of our race—these appetites are a tremendously unruly element in our being as it stands. And to-day we cannot read a newspaper without perceiving that there is a widespread rebellion in all classes of society against the Christian standard of sexual purity. The old-fashioned ignoring of the subject was a very poor substitute for innocency. It is a

102 *Christian Moral Principles*

poor thing, which contrasts very strangely with the open-eyed recognition of facts which we find in the Bible or in Shakespeare. It is indeed perilous to seek to ignore what every grown person knows to be actually going on behind whatever veils of respectability we may throw over it. But at the present day such silence, such ignoring, is no longer anywhere possible. Like a treacherous crust on the surface of a volcano it has broken and let us through. No one can read the newspapers without his eyes finding themselves face to face with widespread rebellion against the Christian standard of what we commonly call morality.[1] Let me name quite simply three points.

S. Paul, when he wrote his epistle to the Corinthians, was writing to people who inhabited what was, I dare say, the most notoriously sensual of the cities of the world. In the place

---

[1] I notice that Lord Mersey, sitting in the Divorce Court, has recently been exposing the claim of "the innocent party" to be called by such a name in the great majority of cases. "I have a strong opinion that these men have nearly all misconducted themselves." And he declared that "it is not in human nature" for men to keep straight, when they are separated from their wives. On this the *Evening News* remarks, "Such a view as that expressed by Lord Mersey will afford small help indeed to a man who may be hesitating on the verge of what not only the Churches but civilized society regards as sin. It would be well did all such remember that their record will come before a greater Judge than the ex-President of the Divorce Court."

The right Self-love

whence he came to Corinth, that is, the famous city of Athens, he found himself in a city wholly given to idolatry; but when he came to Corinth he found himself in a city wholly given to lust. And you remember how he writes to them about the almost universal sin of fornication. He refers to it as a thing which every one who names the name of Christ must regard as a fundamental outrage upon Him to whom he belongs. Now I ask you to contrast with this horror of S. Paul the ordinary assumptions in any class of our society to-day as reflected in common talk or in popular literature, and you will not think I am exaggerating when I speak of a widespread revolt amongst us against the Christian standard of purity, and acknowledge a widespread denial of the very possibility of that which S. Paul affirms to be a primary necessity for any one who bears the name of Christian.

Or take the law of marriage. S. Paul is our earliest witness of what our Lord taught with regard to marriage, and he surely is quite explicit. It admits in certain extreme cases of separation; but not of remarriage while both partners live. So S. Mark, so S. Luke, record our Lord's teaching. I am aware, of course, of the apparent exception introduced into the text of the Gospel of S. Matthew, and though I cannot doubt that our Lord taught the indissolubility of marriage without exception, yet I cannot deny that what seems to be the reasonable interpretation of S. Matthew justifies any national church in adopting the allowance of that single exception. But it does not in any way satisfy the demands of our contemporary society; it does not satisfy even our present civil law. I am not now concerned with what may be possible in any civil society which is not really anxious to maintain its Christian loyalty. I am speaking only of the law for Christians. I say, then, that the law of indissoluble marriage is proclaimed by our earliest witnesses in the New Testament; it was the law of the primitive church; it has been the law of the Western church throughout; it is still the law of our own part of the church, unrepealed and unmistakable, and the presumption of our marriage service. And yet you know how widespread is the rebellion against this severe law in contemporary society.

One other point I must mention. The Bible, reflecting the healthy instincts of mankind, glorifies and rejoices in the large family. The current view of such a family as an intolerable burden is not a healthy view. I think history

The right Self-love

bears witness that the ridicule of fertile parenthood so prevalent to-day is a sign of national declension and decadence.[1] We cannot doubt what would have been the mind and language of S. Paul, nay, may I not say with reverence? what would have been the mind and language of our Lord, if they had been face to face with that misuse of science which to-day provides men and women with artificial preventives of what the Bible, and indeed the healthy instinct of humanity at large, proclaims to be among God's greatest blessings. I know, of course, that the complexities of modern society have introduced great difficulties into the following out of the Christian law of pure living both by hindering marriage and supplying motives for the restriction of the family. I cannot now dwell further upon the subject; but I should like to ask you to make yourselves acquainted with the solemn and sane words which were spoken by the Lambeth Conference of Bishops last year in that part of their report which deals with this particular subject.[2] I would have you read both the report of the Committee which

[1] The recent census in France shows that the population has so decreased that the present Chamber of Deputies should be reduced by ninety members, i.e. on the basis of one member for every 75,000 inhabitants.

[2] The Report, published by S.P.C.K., has had, I believe, an enormous sale.

dealt with marriage and sexual problems and the resolutions passed by the whole body of assembled bishops, resolutions eminently worthy of their high office.

I have spoken of the control of our sexual appetites which the service of our Lord requires of us because it is a manifest difficulty, never felt more acutely than to-day. But our Lord will not let us think that sensuality is worse than uncharitableness or pride or jealousy, which are to be ranked, like sensual sins, among the works of the flesh which we are bound to mortify. To live a really Christian life, whatever be the particular nature of our own personal temptations, is undoubtedly a difficult thing. But, after all, the hardship and difficulty of the Way is not the prevalent thought of the New Testament. The sense of hardship is swallowed up in the sense of joy and power and courage of which the New Testament is full.

The characteristic of the Christian life is liberty. "If the Son maketh you free, ye shall be free indeed." "Where the spirit is Lord, there is liberty."[1] And, as almost all serious moralists have told us, liberty means something much more than the absence of external con-

---

[1] 2 Cor. iii. 17. I believe, with Hort and Chase, that this translation probably represents the original text.

straint, and something quite different from doing what we please. To do what we please is to surrender ourselves to our appetites: and that leads not to liberty, but, as common language warns us, to slavery to our lower nature. That man is certainly not free whose higher nature—his will and reason—is dragged at the chariot wheels of his lusts and passions. Freedom means the power to realize our true being —the power to be what we ought, which is what the Bible means by saving our souls. This is the liberty with which Christ has made us free. In the power of His Spirit I can be what I ought. And the more habitually I remember God; the more habitually I think of Christ who died for me and gives Himself wholly to me in His holy sacrament to renew me, flesh and spirit alike, after His likeness; the more habitually I think of His Spirit dwelling in me— the easier it will be to overcome temptation. Indeed there is no moment of temptation, however acute, when, if I will deliberately turn to God in Christ, and invoke His Spirit who makes my body His temple—crying out in my heart "Holy Spirit, help me"—I shall not find that Holy Spirit's help given me to control my wrong impulses and pour into my heart the sense of redeeming power.

The fact is, so many men live habitually without the sense of God, and are then full of complaints that the Christian standard is impossibly high. It is high but possible; but it is possible only if we will steadily face the fact that we can live to the true only by deliberately dying to the false.

Christ died to sin, S. Paul says. He deliberately refused it and turned His back upon it. That is why the world of sin put Him to death. His death upon the Cross was a death to sin. But thus dying to sin He lives to God. And that law of living through dying—living in the true life by dying to the false—is the law for Christians, as it was the law of Christ's own life. The only way to live the life that is life indeed is to die to the life which disfigures, dishonours, and corrupts our manhood. Even Goethe, though I fear his life was apt to belie his words, yet, intellectually at least, perceived the necessary law.

> "Stirb und werde!
> Gar, so lang du das nicht hast,
> Bist du nur ein trübe Gast
> Auf der dunkeln Erde."

"Die to live! for so long as thou hast not that, thou art but a troubled stranger upon the gloomy earth."

The right Self-love

In this Holy Week you are looking to the Cross. There you see the figure of your great example in whose steps you would walk; there you see the sinfulness of sin which crucified Him; there you see the perfect sacrifice which has won for us the forgiveness of our sins, that is the constant opportunity for a fresh start, free from all the taint and burden of the past; and there also you see, as S. Paul teaches you, the law of your new life. Die to live. And the more deliberately you accept that law, the more resolutely you turn your back upon false ideals of life and welcome with all your soul the "life which is life indeed," the more you will feel the power of the Spirit of Jesus to give you liberty.

APPENDIX

THE TEN COMMANDMENTS IN THE CHRISTIAN CHURCH [1]

In the Prayer Book the Decalogue holds a position of singular importance. It is to be learnt by heart by every baptized person; it is interpreted in the Catechism; it is propounded as the constant standard for self-examination; and, above all, it is recited at every celebration of Holy Communion. Some such position for the Ten Commandments, side by side with the Creed and the Lord's Prayer, is commonly supposed to be primitive and necessary. Thus (in an excellent book) the late Bishop of Manchester writes: "This (the co-ordination of Creed, Lord's Prayer, and Ten Commandments) is the tradition which has come down to us from the early Church. On these lines Cyril of Jerusalem based his Catechetical Lectures"; [2] and (it is implied) on these lines S. Augustine founded his *Manual* or *Enchiridion*. But this is quite a mistake. S. Cyril's Catechetical Lectures [3] and S. Augus-

[1] Reprinted from the author's *Dominant Ideas and Corrective Principles*. (Mowbrays.)

[2] Dr. Knox, *Pastors and Teachers*, p. 82. (Longmans, 1902.)

[3] *Catecheses* vi–xviii are on the Creed. Then the sacraments (mysteries) are explained, and the Lord's Prayer is interpreted in *Cat. Myst.* v. 11–18.

Appendix

tine's Manual [1] and Teaching for Catechumens are based solely on the Creed and the Lord's Prayer. There is no allusion to the Decalogue at all in the former, and in the latter only the briefest.[2] The Creed and the Lord's Prayer were also the only formulas used in the preparation of candidates for baptism.[3] The fact is that till the thirteenth century the Decalogue was not co-ordinated with the Lord's Prayer and the Creed as the summary of moral instruction to be known by all men; nor was it ever used in the Liturgy, nor in the preparation for baptism. The Creed and the Lord's Prayer stood alone in the patristic period. At various dates in the mediaeval period there were added to them, as to be known of all men, the seven deadly sins, the seven principal virtues, the seven sacraments, the angelic salutation. But not till the thirteenth century can I find an instance of the collocation with these of the Ten Commandments.

Of course, from the first it was recognized, as indeed S. Paul and our Lord Himself require it to be recognized, that the Christian moral law is built upon the "Ten Words," and that they have divine authority. This is excellently expressed by Irenaeus: "It was to prepare

[1] *Enchiridion*, c. 2.
[2] Ch. 32—that the Decalogue is summed up in the twofold law of love, cp. *de Catech. Rudibus*, c. 41.
[3] The "instruments of the holy law," which at Rome were solemnly made known to the candidate (as well as the Creed and Lord's Prayer) were the four Gospels, not the Decalogue.

men for the life (of friendship with Himself and concord with their fellows) that the Lord Himself, without any intermediary, spoke the words of the Decalogue to all alike; and therefore likewise they remain in force amongst us, receiving extension and addition, but not dissolution, through His coming in the flesh."[1]

But, in spite of this universal recognition of the divine authority of the Ten Commandments, very little was said about them. It is true that, amidst the jumble of moral precepts which occupy the first six chapters of *The Didache*, which were intended for the instruction of catechumens, six of the Ten Commandments are found; and they occur sporadically in the Patristic writers as was inevitable, often with the remark that they have received their fulfilment in the twofold law of love. But there was not the same need experienced for a formula of morality as for a formula of faith. There was, in fact, no attempt to provide such a formula; and when Origen and Ambrose first attempted a systematic treatment of Christian morals they found a basis for it not in the Ten Commandments, but in the four cardinal virtues recognized in the heathen world—prudence (or wisdom), temperance (or self-control), justice and fortitude (or courage).[2]

[1] *C. haer.* iv. 16, 3, 4.
[2] For Origen, see the account given by Gregory Thaumaturgus, his pupil, of his method in ethics, *Or. Pan.*, c. ix. For Ambrose, see his famous *de Officiis*, and see also S. Augustine *de Moribus Eccl. Cath.* xv. 25.

Appendix

There is thus curiously little about the Ten Commandments in the fathers. Origen and Augustine both indeed discuss the proper method of dividing and distributing the Ten Words. Origen further gives an interesting interpretation of the first two Commandments,[1] and S. Augustine a "spiritual" interpretation of the fourth: "It is not with thee (a Christian) as with the Jews. . . . To thee it is said that thou shouldest observe the Sabbath spiritually by learning the true rest (in God) in hope of the future eternal rest. Rest that thou mayest labour, and labour that thou mayest rest."[2] Later (in the eighth century) in connection with the Iconoclastic controversy, the Second Commandment comes prominently into controversy, and John of Damascus enunciates the principle that the Incarnation — by which God has manifested Himself visibly, to be seen and touched—has made all the difference in its interpretation. "We make images not of the invisible Godhead, but of the visible flesh." For those who cannot read, these images are their reminders—their books.[3] Something, then, there is in the fathers about the Decalogue; but, on the whole, in the patristic period we hear noticeably little of it.

But at least from the time of S. Augustine

---

[1] Origen, *in Exod. Hom.* viii.
[2] *Quaestt. in Heptateuch*, ii. 71.
[3] S. John Damas., *de Imag.* Or. i. 4-17.

114   *Christian Moral Principles*

in the West the idea prevailed that the Decalogue was the republication of the natural law written in men's hearts, which the prevalence of sin had obliterated, and which, therefore, needed reassertion with divine authority as a foundation on which the work of divine redemption might be based.[1] This idea falls in with S. Paul's conception of the function of the Law; and gives it its signal importance as a moral foundation, its prohibitory aspect being explained and justified as a clearing of the ground of the human heart preparatory to its proper normal cultivation.[2]

On this principle the mediaeval scholastics gave greater prominence to the Ten Commandments;[3] and, though they interpreted them very freely in a Christian sense, they insisted on them as a foundation to be known of all men. So it is that they became associated with the Creed and the Lord's Prayer as the formula of moral duty which all must know.

---

[1] See S. Aug., *Enarr. in Ps. lvii.* 1 and *in Ps. cxviii. Serm. xxv.* 4. See also Pseud. Aug. *Quaest. in Vel. Test.* 4 (Migne, *P.L.* xxxv, 2219): "Lex formata in litteris dari non debuit quia in natura ipsa quodam modo inserta est . . . at ubi naturalis lex evanuit, oppressa consuetudine delinquendi, tunc opportuit legem manifestari, ut in Judaeis omnes homines audirent." Cf. Eucherius of Lyons (fifth cent.), *P.L.* l. 780; Alcuin, *P.L.*, c. 518; Hildebert, *P.L.* clxxi. 1148: "Lex data ut repararet legem naturalem." Hugo of S. Victor, *P.L.* clxxvi. 420, etc.

[2] See Rupert de Deutz, *P.L.* clxvii. 680: "Hic in initio non iam charitas imperatur, sed quae contraria sunt charitati prohibentur, ut in illis exstirpatis tum demum ipsa charitas radix omnium bonorum substituatur."

[3] S. Thomas Aquinas *Summa Theol.* 2ᵃ, 2ᵃᵉ, qu. c.

Appendix

So it is that for the first time (as far as I can discern) in the constitution of Bishop de Kirkham of Durham (1255) and the Synodal Statutes of Norwich (1257) the following injunction appears.[1] "Therefore, because without the observance of the Decalogue there can be no salvation of souls, we exhort and enjoin in the Lord that every pastor of souls and every parish priest should know the Decalogue, that is the ten precepts of the Mosaic law, and should frequently preach and explain the same to the people who are under his control. Let him know also the seven heads of wrong-doing (*septem criminalia*), and preach to the people the avoidance of the same. Let him know in like manner the seven sacraments of the Church, and let those who are priests know particularly the things necessary for the sacrament of true confession and penance, and let them frequently teach the laity in the common tongue the form of baptizing. Let each of them have also a simple knowledge of the Faith as it is contained in the Creeds, both the greater (Nicene) and the lesser (Apostles') and in the tract which is called *Quicunque Vult*, which is sung daily at Prime." Kirkham adds to the requirements of elementary religious instruction the Lord's Prayer and the angelic salutation of Mary and the knowledge of how to make the sign

[1] See Wilkins's *Concilia* i. 704, 731. There are only minor differences.

of the cross. More explicitly and fully Archbishop Peckham in 1281, in his constitution, "Ignorantia Sacerdotum,"[1] ordains "that every parish priest four times a year, that is once every quarter, on one or more days of solemn observance, shall expound to the people in the vulgar tongue, without the fantastic concealment of any kind of subtlety, the fourteen[2] Articles of Faith, the Ten Commandments of the Decalogue, the two precepts of the Gospel, that is the double law of love, the seven works of mercy, the seven capital sins with their offspring, the seven principal virtues, and the seven sacraments of grace." And to take away all excuse of ignorance from the clergy, he enumerates all those necessary rudiments of spiritual knowledge and gives a Christian explanation of the Ten Commandments, to help the clergy in explaining them. I think it is worth while to translate it without any criticism.

"Of the Ten Commandments of the Old Testament three refer to God, which are called the commandments of the first table, and seven to our neighbours, which are called the commandments of the second table. In the first (i.e. our i and ii) is prohibited all idolatry, where it is said *Thou shalt have no other gods in My presence.* Therein

[1] Wilkins, ii. 54. This constitution was repeated in the Province of York, finally by Cardinal Wolsey, in 1518. Wilkins iii, 662, 664 f.

[2] The Articles of the Creeds were so reckoned.

implicitly are prohibited all divinations and charms with the superstitious observance of marks and such figments. In the second, where it is said *Thou shalt not take the Name of the Lord thy God in vain*, is prohibited principally heresy of all kinds, and secondarily all blasphemy and irreverent use of the Name of God, especially in false swearing. In the third commandment, where it is said *Remember to keep the Sabbath holy*, there is enjoined worship according to the Christian religion ('cultus religionis Christianae'), to which clergy and laity alike are bound. Wherefore it should be known that the obligation to observe the legal Sabbath, according to the form of the Old Testament, ceased altogether with the other ceremonies of the law, and there succeeded to it under the New Testament the mode of abstaining from work for the purpose of divine worship ('vacandi cultui divino') on the Lord's Day and other solemn days appointed for this purpose by the authority of the Church: on such days the manner of abstaining from work is not to be taken from the Jewish superstitions but from the canonical injunctions.

"The first commandment of the second table is *Honour thy father and thy mother*, in which it is explicitly commanded to honour parents temporally and spiritually; but implicitly and secondarily every man, according to what his position requires, is to be honoured in accordance with the same commandment. And in the commandment father and mother are to be understood not only according to the flesh but also spiritually, so that the 'father' is any officer of the Church, mediate or immediate; and the 'mother' is the Church whose sons all Catholics are. The second is *Thou shalt not kill*, in which is explicitly forbidden any unpermitted destruction of a person by consent or act or word or favour; and implicitly is here forbidden every unjust harming of any person. So they murder in the spiritual sense who do not sustain the needy; they murder in the civil sense who destroy the character of others ('qui detrahunt'), or who oppress and confound[1] the innocent. The third commandment is *Thou shalt not commit adultery*, in which explicitly adultery is forbidden, but implicitly fornication, which is explicitly forbidden in Deuteronomy xxii. In the same commandment is forbidden all sexual connection not covered by marriage, and all kinds of voluntary pollution. The fourth commandment is *Thou shalt not steal*, in which is explicitly forbidden all secret dealing with another's goods against his will; implicitly all injurious treatment of another's goods, whether by fraud or usury or violence or terrorism. The fifth commandment is *Thou shalt not bear false witness*, wherein is expressly forbidden false witness intended to hurt another: implicitly false witness intended to promote an unworthy person contrary to his deserts. In this commandment all lying, especially to another's hurt, is forbidden. The sixth commandment is *Thou shalt not covet thy neighbour's house*: supply 'to his injury': in which is explicitly forbidden the

[1] Or "cause to stumble" ("offendant").

Appendix 119

coveting of all immovable property, especially what belongs to any Catholic. The seventh commandment is *Thou shalt not desire thy neighbour's wife* or manservant or maidservant or ox or ass or anything that is his, in all of which the coveting of any movable property is forbidden."

It then goes on to expound the twofold law of love which the Gospel has "added" to the Ten Commandments—bidding men, amongst other things, to love each and every man more than all temporal wealth ("affluentiam")—and the seven works of mercy and the seven principal virtues—faith, hope, charity, prudence, justice, temperance, fortitude—and the seven sacraments. Let this suffice as a specimen of rudimentary moral instruction from the heart of the middle age.

Thus in the thirteenth century the Decalogue came to be conjoined with the Creed, the Lord's Prayer, and the seven sacraments as constituting the necessary rudiments for every Christian man. Thus, in 1566, the Catechism of the Council of Trent[1] is able to say that "our ancestors most wisely distributed the whole sum and substance of Christian doctrine under those four heads—the Apostles' Creed, the Sacraments, the Decalogue, the Lord's Prayer." And when the Reformation came, though the teaching about the sacraments was

[1] Proem. xii. The statement would be true of the three previous centuries, not of the earlier period.

modified and their number was reduced to two, still the Reformers retained the Decalogue with the Creed, the Lord's Prayer and the Sacraments as the constituent elements in the Catechisms which contained the necessary doctrine for all Christians. So it was in Luther's two Catechisms of 1530 and 1539, and in Calvin's Catechism of 1535, and in the Heidelberg Catechism of 1563, and substantially (though the Creed is not mentioned) in the Shorter Catechism of the Westminster Assembly (1647).[1] So it was in our English *Institution of a Christian Man* (1537) and *A necessary Doctrine and Erudition for any Christian Man* (1543), with some subsidiary topics added. So of course it is in our Prayer Book Catechism.[2] As for the recitation of the Commandments in the service of Holy Communion, precedent for this was found in the practice which followed upon the injunctions of Archbishop Peckham, and the like practice in other countries. There are also closer precedents of the Reformation period which have been suggested. But this is hardly the place to discuss the question further.[3] It is obvious that when once the Ten Commandments have been accepted as a summary state-

[1] Many of these Catechisms are to be found in the Appendix to Knox's *Pastors and Teachers*.

[2] In its first form the Catechism was perhaps unique among the manuals of the period in containing no treatment of the sacraments. Brightman, *English Rite* (Rivingtons), p. cxxii.

[3] It is discussed by Brightman, *The English Rite*, pp. clvii f., 1039 f. ; also by Scudamore, *Notitia Eucharistica*, pp. 224 f.

Appendix

ment of our moral obligations, just as the Creed is for our Credenda, the recital of the one is as natural as the recital of the other in the service of the altar, and the Commandments form a natural basis for a penitential preparation.

At the same time I cannot feel that we can acquiesce in our present use of the Decalogue in the preparatory portion of our liturgy as satisfactory.

The fact that the Decalogue represents an early stage of the divine law, and that before it can reach the level of Christ's teaching it needs to be profoundly spiritualized and interpreted, seems to make it questionable whether it should be so constantly and nakedly propounded as the summary of the moral law to Christian people. If we are to have the divine prohibitions constantly thundered over us, it would seem as if we should have them in the form in which they apply to ourselves rather than in the form in which they were given to the people of Israel at a very early stage of its education.

No doubt the reiterated "Thou shalt not" has been very impressive. But what are the things which in the Decalogue are explicitly prohibited? The Second Commandment prohibits the making of any image or representation of God, and as it stands it ignores the difference which has been made by the Incarnation. The Fourth Commandment in its literal sense, so far as concerns the observance of the Sabbath, has been abrogated, and is valid only in a "mystical" sense.[1] The Third Commandment requires very fundamental deepening before (as our Lord seems to teach us) we get down through it to the universal duty of truthfulness. The Sixth and Seventh Commandments prohibit only murder and adultery, and require an interpretation which is not always present to the mind before they can be taken to prohibit all unkindness and lawless sensual indulgence of all kinds.

Thus the constant recitation of the Commandments without note or comment has, I cannot but feel, created in part a false conscience amongst our people, and in part condoned much too slack a conscience. No doubt these Ten Commandments have been interpreted in the statements of our duty to God and our duty to our neighbour in the Catechism, but the interpretation is not much in the mind of the people, and it is not by them connected with the particular Commandments. Moreover, it can hardly be denied that the insistence in the "Duty towards my neighbour," upon obedience to superiors and humility and reverence to "betters" (which word certainly means those above us in social station) is not sufficiently balanced by an equal insistence upon the duties of the stronger towards the weaker and the true principles

[1] The Scottish Office, 1637: "According to the mystical meaning of the said commandment."

Appendix

of Christian equality and brotherliness. I cannot but think that the kind of criticism which is commonly heard of the "Duty towards my neighbour," as tending "to keep the people down," and as being "in favour of the upper classes," though it is often accompanied with a misquotation ("that state of life unto which it *has pleased* God to call me," instead of "that state of life unto which it *shall please* God to call me") has yet a good deal of justification.

Thus (1) I would have the Church cease from the *constant* recitation of the Commandments at the beginning of the service of Holy Communion. (2) I would have them occasionally recited, as Archbishop Peckham enjoined, with an interpretation like his, in the full Christian spirit. (3) I would have the interpretation in the Catechism so modified as to be more impartial and to express more adequately the true principle of the equal worth of every soul in God's sight. It is obvious that any Christian interpretation of the Commandments drawn up by authority would, because it was Christian, be more positive and less negative than the Decalogue as it stands.

Printed by A. R. Mowbray & Co. Ltd., London and Oxford

By the Right Rev. CHARLES GORE, D.D., D.C.L., LL.D., lately Bishop of Oxford.

Eighth Impression, completing Forty Thousand.

THE RELIGION OF THE CHURCH.
As presented in the Church of England. A Manual of Membership. 1s. 6d. net; Cloth, 3s. net.

"Will receive a warm welcome not only for its author's sake, but also for the special purpose he has in view."—*The Times.*

"Brevity, simplicity of style, boldness and clearness in exposition or investigation, freedom from such over-restraint as often comes from official caution, frankness in stating the duties of membership and in suggesting measures of reform, are all marks which will go to make the book of service to the average member of the Church."—*Challenge.*

"Dr. Gore has done an immense service by endeavouring, in his own words, to 'meet a need which is just now clamorous—the provision of a manual of instruction for the members of the Church of England.'"—*Church Times.*

Third Impression.

DOMINANT IDEAS AND CORRECTIVE PRINCIPLES
Cloth, 3/6 net.

"In these pages we have, if we may say so, Dr. Gore in his happiest manner, with its old combination of balanced judgement, restrained enthusiasm, and obvious sincerity."—*Guardian.*

Second Impression.

THE FALL OF MAN.
A Sermon preached in substance in Balliol College Chapel on January 30, and in S. Paul's Cathedral on February 13, 1921. 6d. net.

In this sermon Dr. Gore treats of the Church's doctrine of the Fall, and shows how its truth remains unaffected by the discoveries of science and of Biblical criticism.

STEPS TOWARDS UNITY.
Being an Address delivered at Kingsway Hall. 6d. net.

Second Impression.

DR. HEADLAM'S BAMPTON LECTURES.
An Open Letter to the Bishop of Nassau. 6d. net.

A. R. MOWBRAY & CO. LTD., LONDON AND OXFORD

www.ingramcontent.com/pod-product-compliance
Lightning Source LLC
Chambersburg PA
CBHW070502100426
42743CB00010B/1726